CONTENTS

ISBN-13: 9781527276376
ISBN-10: 1527276376

Cover design by: Art Painter
Library of Congress Control Number: 2018675309
Printed in the United States of America

To Nicky. Always the fire in my heart.

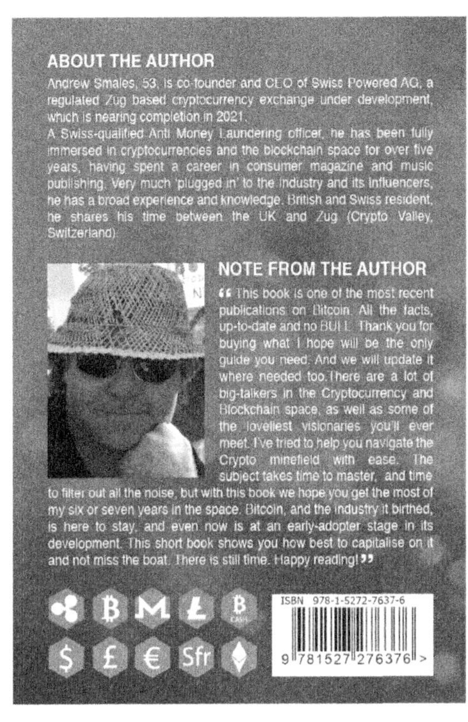

ABOUT THE AUTHOR

Andrew Smales, 53, is co-founder and CEO of Swiss Powered AG, a regulated Zug based cryptocurrency exchange under development, which is nearing completion in 2021.
A Swiss-qualified Anti Money Laundering officer, he has been fully immersed in cryptocurrencies and the blockchain space for over five years, having spent a career in consumer magazine and music publishing. Very much 'plugged in' to the industry and its influencers, he has a broad experience and knowledge. British and Swiss resident, he shares his time between the UK and Zug (Crypto Valley, Switzerland).

NOTE FROM THE AUTHOR

"This book is one of the most recent publications on Bitcoin. All the facts, up-to-date and no BULL. Thank you for buying what I hope will be the only guide you need. And we will update it where needed too.There are a lot of big-talkers in the Cryptocurrency and Blockchain space, as well as some of the loveliest visionaries you'll ever meet. I've tried to help you navigate the Crypto minefield with ease. The subject takes time to master, and time to filter out all the noise, but with this book we hope you get the most of my six or seven years in the space. Bitcoin, and the industry it birthed, is here to stay, and even now is at an early-adopter stage in its development. This short book shows you how best to capitalise on it and not miss the boat. There is still time. Happy reading!"

ISBN 978-1-5272-7637-6
9 781527 276376 >

1. INTRODUCTION (6 MIN READ)

"Bitcoin is a remarkable cryptographic achievement and the ability to create something that is not duplicable in the digital world has enormous value."
Eric Schmidt, ex Google CEO.

On January 3, 2009, in the aftermath of the financial crash, The Times, London, ran the headline "Chancellor on brink of second bailout for banks". In the middle of this chaos, Bitcoin had just booted up for the first time. The first of these electronic coins, minted by its mysterious founder, contained the headline in its code as proof of inception. Nobody would ever put the genie back in the bottle.

A couple of months after that, Bitcoin was three a penny, worth a mere $0.003, meaning you could have bought yourself over 33,000 for less than $100. By November 2020, those bitcoins would be worth nearly 500 million dollars. Had you invested $1000, you would be a billionaire more than four times over. But don't despair just yet. I missed the early years too, and we really aren't too late. In fact, things are only just getting revved up. Bitcoin really is real, and I'm going to prove it to you.

The technology that Bitcoin and other cryptocurrencies brought to the world is called Blockchain. It is upending the way many industries are run, especially the entire banking and 'money' sector, for which it is particularly well suited.

I hear you, I hear you "But it's too late for me to get into Bitcoin now isn't it?". There is no need to worry, because Bitcoin is now well on track to become a new world reserve currency. The technology it gave us is changing many aspects of our lives already. Besides, there are plenty of other exciting coins and projects, many of which have, at times, outperformed Bitcoin from a purely market-value standpoint. There are a fair few duff ones too, unfortunately, but I'll do my best to tell you how to avoid them. With any new technology there are bad players also. Always. And Crypto is undoubtedly no exception.

But now, many large organisations, investment firms and well-known individuals, are putting hundreds of millions of dollars of their capital into Bitcoin. Many have wholly U-turned from their initially scathing comments. It's the coolest thing on Wall Street right now. It sits comfortably alongside traditional assets like gold and stocks and easily outperforms them all. Despite the 'alternate facts' that Bitcoin is only used by criminals, in fact only 2% of transactions are thought to be illicit. Compare that with cash-money, at 15% illegal use, which is nearly ten times as much.

This book tells the full true-story, while nailing the basics, with a minimum of jargon for jargon's sake. Hopefully, as if we were just chatting and discussing it over a cup of coffee. Even if you already know a bit, this book will complete the picture for you.

Twelve years in, and Bitcoin is still in relative infancy and growing all the time. Whether you buy a whole one or a tiny fraction, you can always have skin in the game. This 'game' is all about the best performing asset ever. Even though 2019 was a relatively slow year, by December 2020, it had tripled in price year-on-year. Plus it's now far more stable, price-wise, than it's ever been. You don't have the wild swings and panic any more. These are the signs of a maturing asset with real market support. Its smart design, combining elements of cryptography and economic theory, is there to make it increase in value over time. We will contrast this to our Pounds, Dollars and Euros, which reduce in value due to inflation and money-printing, especially at times of economic crisis. Like right now.

Since that day in January 2009, thousands of cryptocurrencies have been released. Many are just cloned or altered versions of Bitcoin, most are centralised, some are inevitable scams. But a select few have truly promising use-case scenarios. A basic but fundamental understanding of the technology, not to mention the bullshit, is essential to navigate without running aground. Then you can objectively pin down the winners from the losers and understand the opportunities.

Mastering the basics can be, at first, a challenging path. It's not something that can be done in a quick conversation or web search, and it's not enough to just accept what we're told. There's no 30-second elevator-pitch here. A lot of it is smoke and mirrors too, from people who will happily fleece you for everything you have and give nothing back in return. Rule number one; if you don't understand something, don't move forward until you do. If the 24-year-old in front of you seems like an unfeasibly young genius, don't worry. Stop and think. Nowhere is this more important than Cryptocurrencies. It's too easy to be embarrassed into a corner simply because the tech sounds so smart, but maybe isn't, and just go along with it. There's no shame in saying "hang on a minute" or "excuse me, what the bloody hell are you talking about" because half the time you'd probably be right. They'll be talking 97% bullshit or, at best, regurgitating one crypto-cliché after another. Thankfully there are plenty of hard-working innovators in this space too, which hopefully you should subsequently be able to spot. And I certainly won't shame you just for wanting to learn, to show how clever I am. It's a fascinating world, one I became quickly immersed in, obsessed with really, and hopefully you will too.

The genius of Bitcoin is its technical and economics concepts, and these are initially hard to extract from all the noise surrounding Cryptocurrencies. But I've been through that 'pain' years ago (I loved it) and the ideas have since been brewed into my brain. So herein, only facts, not fiction. All the information and grounding you need is here and will unfold in this book. And I've tried hard not to waffle on, so it won't take you a week to read either. Well, with that said, I'd better get on with it, hadn't I. You don't need to be a technical genius, but gaining a solid foundation has never been more critical in any field. After that, everything comes easily. That's a promise.

Andrew Smales, Zug (Crypto Valley), Switzerland, November 2020

2. THE ORIGINS AND REALITY OF MONEY

"It is no co-incidence that the century of total war coincided with the century of central banking."
Ron Paul, End The Fed.

Ever since us homo sapiens arrived on earth about 300,000 years ago, the concept of 'money' has changed little. Its fundamental purpose is as a medium of exchange. So as long as it retained value in the real world, and was trusted, then who was to say what was and what wasn't money.

In around 9,000 BC cattle were first domesticated. Accordingly, cows, camels, sheep and goats naturally became a unit of exchange through bartering. You might swap a chicken for a bushel of apples, or a reindeer pelt for a flint weapon or anything else of intrinsic value. Not that you could stuff a sheep in your pocket and go about your daily business. Of course, some of the earliest forms of money were jewellery and beads. These were often made with valuable metals, stones and minerals. In fact, gold flakes have been found in caves dating back as far as 40,000 BC. The amount of time taken to make these objects of desire, and the elements they contained, denoted their value. So time and effort are used as a concept to express value as well. The more time spent, the greater the value. As such, until the process was simplified or industrialised, their value usually went up as time went on. And, of course, jewellery is a particularly beautiful way to store wealth, as it is to this day.

As early as 500AD, people in Micronesia used carved Rai stones to represent real value. These large hand-carved disc-shaped stones, with a hole in the middle, were sometimes as large as four metres in diameter. Even less portable than sheep. Villagers often travelled miles in small boats to remote locations and other islands to dig up the stone. The rarer, the better. Then thousands of man-hours were spent creating them. Because the resulting Rai could sometimes be too heavy to move, they often remained in place in front of the village hall, or at meeting places and along pathways. Ownership was simply transferred from person to person.

Eventually, and for centuries, humankind moved to other, more portable, ways to store value. And these days we call these 'Fiat' currencies. Fiat, in Latin, stands for 'It shall be done', meaning that the money was a means to an end and medium of exchange. "I shall give you this coin in exchange for your goods or services. It shall be done". The earliest recorded coins were in Greece in around 600 BC. The Drachma, similarly meaning 'to grasp' was initially made with electrum, an alloy of gold and silver, which is how it is discovered in the ground. This had real value. But in time, that value was eroded as the metals used were mixed with cheaper alloys, until eventually the coins contained no gold at all. After that, history teaches us that faith in the value of the coin will ultimately disappear and when confidence in its value is universally lost, the Fiat currency is dead.

All Fiat currencies have ended this way. It sometimes takes time (sometimes not), but it does happen. The Chinese used bronze shells called 'Cowrie-coins' from at least 1500BC, progressing naturally to coins from around 500 BC., to notes in 960 AD., but these too were not to last indefinitely. Today the British Pound Sterling is currently far-and-away the oldest, still-existing, currency in the world, effectively born in 775 AD. This is, incredibly, a millennia before the US dollar, which was released in 1792. The Euro, meanwhile, is still an infant, at just over 20 years old. Don't worry, it's trying hard to make up for it and inflating fast. The ECB can't print money fast enough, and it's not you or me that benefits, that's for sure. There are over 180 Fiat currencies in use in the world today. Historically none (yes none) have survived in the long term due to contemporary economic policies. Even the super stable Swiss Franc is only 222 years old.

The main problem is that they rely on a promise, usually from a government or central bank, that the value will remain, while simultaneously having zero intrinsic or 'real' value. Left alone, this system could theoretically work well, if that simple promise meant anything, even though they're just pieces of paper. But all governments adjust the money supply according to their financial needs, defence budgets, etc. Central banks, which are run by private bankers anyway, support them in times of war or peace. Usually war. And at a significant profit, of course. Just to reiterate that; yes, the central banks are privately owned 'for-profit' organisations, and charge your government for the privilege of printing 'money' out of thin air. On bits of paper, and effectively appearing out of nowhere on their balance sheet. The general public is none the wiser about how much money is produced. This means that the diluted cash in your pocket can *only* be worth less. No wonder that, in the late 18th century, Mayer Amschel Rothschild, founder of the private banking dynasty, said: "Permit me to issue and control the money of a nation, and I care not who makes its laws". That's precisely what they got to do. They have owned the money-go-round ever since, and milked it for their own benefit for a hundred years. But still that isn't enough to satiate their greed for power and money. The cycle is like a black hole that would eat itself if it could. Thankfully, and thanks to Bitcoin, that balance of power is about to change.

And so it came to pass, that in 2020, to temporarily stave off economic collapse in the wake of Covid-19, but basically to give yet more money to the already-rich, the US Federal Reserve printed, or let's say minted, 22% of all US dollars ever produced in the entire history of the currency. That's 9 trillion dollars, or almost $30,000 per person. Out of thin air. In a year. This cannot end well. You would be quite crazy to hold dollars for anything other than short term use. In this climate, Fiat money becomes worth less and less daily. You can't even earn interest on it any more, which says it all. In Switzerland and Germany, where I work, we have to actually pay to hold cash in the bank due to negative interest rates (0.2% and 0.4% respectively). It's true. I even get an annual fee from the holding-deposit for the office I rent in Zug, because the amount decreases gradually. For merely keeping it in a bank. Coming soon, to a country near you! And yes, you're right, it can't possibly work. So recently, this unsurprising lack of confidence in the value of money, by the very institutions themselves too, by the way, left pretty much just the stock market for people to invest in. That partly explains its meteoric, but in the view of many, unsustainable, rise.

If further proof of the Fiat swindle was needed, consider this example. After the first world war, the German currency, the Mark, became hyper-inflated due to wartime borrowing diluting its value. And then some. War is very expensive, and can only be financed out of fresh air, don't forget. Consequently, so hyper was the inflation that ensued, it actually became cheaper to burn stacks of paper money than to buy wood with it. This collapse led to dreadful poverty and the rise of fascism-on-speed a decade later. America too would suffer a four-year vacuum of economic collapse, starting in 1929. Don't worry, the central bankers didn't starve. Stock speculators jumped out of windows, but that's just business. This is what paper money is. Paper.

More recently we have seen hyperinflation on a massive scale around the world, from Venezuela to South Sudan, Argentina, Yugoslavia and Zimbabwe. By the beginning of 2019, inflation in Venezuela had reached a *million* per cent. Zimbabwe, too, ended up issuing 20 trillion-dollar notes, which became worth less than a single US dollar. Hungary holds the record for the largest denomination of a single note where, in 1946, the government printed a 100 quintillion (1020) pengő to keep up. In Lebanon, during the early weeks of the Covid-19 crisis, citizens vandalised bank offices after their currency was devalued. In the aftermath of the last global collapse in 2009, Cypress took 50% of its citizens' funds - directly out of the banks. Imagine that. It's the people that suffer here, but cryptocurrencies offer a real alternative and true independence from all this… nonsense.

In some nations, money in their pocket becomes so devalued, so fast, from government money printing, that poverty and chaos ensue. Now even Cuba is devaluing its Peso too. Don't think "this couldn't happen here" because history shows us that it can, has, and does. And, as we have seen, the US Dollar itself has inflated by 22% in 2020 alone. The start of a 'j-curve'? Many think so. Put it this way, for a few years now you haven't been able to buy oil and gas from Moscow with US dollars.

They want gold. Real gold. On a train. Which is even sillier. Mercifully, there *is* a better way. Meltdown might merely be just around the corner for many of us. Still, people stuck in some of these countries immediately need that alternative to the current state-controlled money system, as do the 1.7 billion unbanked individuals in the world. Incredibly, two-thirds of these people own a mobile phone. That's well over a *billion* new people that could have access to electronic money too. Is that not revolutionary on a giant scale?

Many people still think that government money is backed by real assets like gold, but it isn't. Not anywhere. Governments often only have single-digit percentages of gold compared to the paper money that is in supply. Previously gold was indeed stored 1:1 with the printed cash, and this was called the gold standard in the US. When Roosevelt outlawed private ownership of gold in 1933 (yes, that happened), people were faced with jail or up to a $100,000 fine, by today's standards. Those who turned it in were paid the official price for it of $20.66 per troy ounce. Immediately afterwards, he re-set the price of gold to $35. Cheeky monkey.

The British Pound Sterling originally denoted a pound lb (in weight) of silver. It will now buy you less than 3 grams of the metal, which perfectly illustrates the inflation issue. And since the turn of the 20th century, it has lost over 97% of its value. The gold-standard promise was that the money was pegged against the reserves of gold held in a vault, and you could always get that value back. Even then, though, it was a partial myth. It didn't mean you could go and chip off a bit off a bar in Fort Knox, if indeed there is any significant gold at Fort Knox (but that's another story). Nor did it mean that the government would honour this exchange for sure anyway, how could they? Not your vault, not your gold!

The banks are no better. Their vaults aren't filled with gold either, or money, or anything of value. At least nothing that belongs to them anyway. Because of fractional reserves, they're only required to hold less than 10% of the money *we* have paid in. This varies by country, but all are under that figure. Thanks to covid, some countries have allowed this to drop to zero, just to keep flowing what little money is left. There has yet to be a run on the banks in the west, but it would be very enlightening for all to see what happened if people just started withdrawing their money at the same time. The old system was, and is, entirely built on trust. And it's fair to say that this trust has been eroding away for years if not decades. Unfortunately a fair majority have had their fingers in our ears all their lives, screaming "It'll be alright. La, la, la, la, la, la, la" or "999% APR, um, oh sure, I suppose that doesn't sound too bad, I can always get another loan to pay this one-off". When did that become the norm? You couldn't make it up. We mustn't make the same mistakes with Crypto.

The 'gold standard' in the US was eventually abandoned by Richard Nixon in 1971. And so began a massive money printing exercise that has never ceased, fuelling, at the time, the excesses of the Vietnam War. Ron Paul, quoted above, is 'dead' right about that one. The war cost $188 billion then, or approximately $94,000 per body. That's about a trillion dollars in today's money. That kind of money has to come from somewhere. Oh wait, no it doesn't, just pretend it never happened. This uncontrolled dilution of the money supply is partly responsible for the economy regularly crashing every decade or so. Boom. Then bust. With no need to back it with a 'real' asset, there is no limit to how much money can be printed. And we citizens are none the wiser. "I promise to pay the bearer on demand, the sum of £10" is printed on a British 'Pavarotti' (slang for a tenner). Still, it's also not actually backed by anything, meaning that its real-world value fluctuates. In time it too could become worthless, or at least worth *less*, and we the public have no say over the ongoing wizardry within. At some level we can trust our government maybe? But they're trousering our money. Counterfeiting it at will really.

Like most people, you may be satisfied that our money has everyday value, which, short-term, it temporarily does. However, wouldn't it be wonderful if we could do more. If we could design a better money system that was completely independent of governments or central banks (or *any* banks). One where the value gradually increased instead of decreasing. One which had none of their financial burden of expenditure, or plain greed, and one not subject to devaluation via their infinite money printing. One which has no boss. One which doesn't enable war. Is that too much to ask? After all, we pay our taxes for all of that other stuff, don't we?

That long-overdue money system is Bitcoin.

3. WHAT IS BITCOIN AND CRYPTOCURRENCY?

"Commerce on the Internet has come to rely almost exclusively on financial institutions serving as trusted third parties to process electronic payments."
Satoshi Nakamoto, October 31, 2008.

At the height of the financial crisis in October of 2008, just a month after Lehman Brothers collapsed, an anonymous programmer, or team of programmers, released an academic 'white paper' heralding a brand-new idea. It was called "Bitcoin: A Peer-to-Peer Electronic Cash System". He (or they) went by the pseudonym Satoshi Nakamoto, whose identity has never been revealed to this day. The paper explains a brand-new system of peer-to-peer (person-to-person) money. This money could be transferred almost instantly anywhere in the world. Without the need for any trusted third party like a bank, and at a far lower cost than before. Its architecture ensured that it was both extremely secure while also solving several problems that had previously stood in the way of creating such a currency. After all, why involve a middle-man at all if you don't have to. Me to you. Peer to peer.

Bitcoin is deliberately computer-intensive to create, limited in supply forever (rare), and offers certainty about security. It really does. And say we ran out of gold. The price would rocket, and so it is with Bitcoin. This is not the first time people have tried to create electronic money, but all other attempts, though valiant, have essentially failed. Satoshi well and truly cracked it though. Bitcoin is now being accepted as money by millions (yes millions) of companies and individuals, with thousands more joining in every day. It may 'only' be electronic money, as if that somehow discredits it as money. Still, money is, and always has been, a 'medium of exchange'. Bitcoin does that job, and it does it better, faster, cheaper and more securely than any other form of money in history. It's also an excellent long-term store of wealth, for what it's worth. Or at least it's *designed* that way.

You might not believe me just yet, and that's okay. *But*, it's very, very smart, and a lot more 'real' than pieces of paper. There are several good reasons why, aside from the economic ones. Don't worry if it all isn't crystal clear by the end of the next paragraph. There are other elements that we need to discuss, which we will in the next couple of chapters. If I could, I would explain them simultaneously, but that's the challenge with the subject. So I've broken it up a bit. Everything will become clear. I've promised, remember.

To realise his vision, Satoshi devised an ingenious system whereby the record of all Bitcoin transactions *ever* would not be held centrally. They are distributed across thousands of identical copies which have essentially been put in the hands of the public. Duplicate copies of this data are stored on thousands of 'nodes' (computers) all over the world. The computer code is open-source and free to all. This is called a distributed ledger, and we go into a bit more detail on that in the next chapter. It's this distributed, or *decentralised* nature that makes it such an elegant solution. Not to mention, making it un-hackable. It seems almost obvious now, as do all good ideas in retrospect. Bitcoin is controlled and verified by the actions of many people, not by a few wealthy individuals. Okay, there are a few wealthy individuals. But hopefully they're a bit different from the last lot of wealthy individuals. Nevertheless, they still have no control or power over Bitcoin. Just a voice, like the rest of the community, and a joint vested interest in the health of Bitcoin.

The term Satoshi used to describe this direct person-to-person system was 'trust-less'. This means that you don't have to rely on *anyone* else and can conduct business safely. It can be done in an immutable manner, using only the technology and network. The term trust-less is one of a few slightly confusing misnomers in this space that we'll cover. It can easily be misread as 'you can't trust this', which isn't helpful. Although it could be interpreted as 'no trust' (bad), it means 'no trust *needed*' (good). Without the need to rely on any third-party, Bitcoin can be democratic, open and decentralised, without any interference from anyone. Oh, and unstoppable.

Bitcoin thus became the world's first Cryptocurrency, although Satoshi himself did not, in fact, come up with the word 'cryptocurrency'. An early Bitcoin user did, and Satoshi decided to adopt the term himself. Cryptocurrency literally means 'currency' secured with 'cryptography'. Cryptographic techniques for data encryption are not new; the earliest example is found in an Egyptian tomb, originating c.1900 BC. High-speed electrical communication worldwide was started by the Morse electrical network, which is a direct application of simple cryptography. And, of course, we all know the story of Alan Turing breaking Adolph's Enigma message-encryption machines during the second world war. These are just a couple of the origin stories.

That abbreviation 'Crypto' originally comes from Cryptography, not Cryptocurrencies, though it's impossible not to use it for the latter. Cryptographers have been around for a few more centuries, so I'm not going to deliberately hurt their feelings and argue the toss. After all, they deserve credit for the tech. Remember this; 'crypt-o-graphy' is 'hidden-words'. And crypt-o-currency, of course, is hidden-money.

Another hallmark characteristic of Bitcoin is the fact that the currency is specifically designed to be deflationary. That is to say, worth more over time. This is a stroke of economics genius. The supply of Bitcoins is set in stone in the code as a maximum of 21 million, each one divisible by 100 million so-called 'Satoshis'. So there can never be any more made without consensus. With no money printing to devalue it (*inflate* the supply), and if adoption increases, Bitcoin will become more and more valuable. More and more scarce. Bitcoin's code is so agile that it automatically adjusts the difficulty to compute on the Blockchain, directly triggered by public supply and demand. Fiat currencies (£, $, € etc.) are always inflationary, which means they will always drop in value over time. There is no set ceiling on the amount that can be produced, nor is there a limit to the greed of central bankers or the budgetary demands of the central government. Never has that been truer than now. On the face of it, the word 'deflationary' sounds like the value will deflate, but the opposite is the case. We are talking about deflating the *supply*, not the value. Just as, conversely, inflating or increasing the supply of Fiat currency has resulted in economic *in*flation and *de*valuation. It's the number in circulation that counts – the simple market economics of supply and demand.

Imagine a city with 21 million inhabitants. Shanghai, in fact, has grown to this unfathomable population, actually 24.28 million people. Up from 1 million at the turn of the 20th century, and just under 6 million in 1980. Apologies, that's not relevant to our subject, but the numbers always stagger me. Well if every person there bought one Bitcoin, there would be none left for the rest of Shanghai, let alone the rest of the world. This illustrates the potential future shortage of Bitcoin to go around and how starving the supply could increase value. That said, there are enough Satoshis (hundred-millionth of a bitcoin) for every human in the world to own 269,410 Satoshis each, or 0.00269% of a Bitcoin. This is one of the things that make the coin so malleable going forward. In fact, China banned Bitcoin in September 2017, so the extra potential there is still to be factored into the value. All 24.28 million in wealthy Shanghai *and* the rest of China's 1.4 billion souls. If they want it, they'll find a way to get it. Despite 'the Great Firewall of China', there are ways in and out. The same goes for India, and its massive population too. As demand increases, as it has steadily for twelve years now, the theory goes that the price can only go up in the long run. There are currently over 18.5 million Bitcoins in circulation already. With just 2.5 million more to produce - ever - the free-market has decided its value, which so far has continued to rise, along with its popularity. Remember, money is just a 'medium of exchange' or 'store of value'. Bitcoin is arguably both. It may not be quite as agile as some of its newcomer altcoins, but it's secure and universally trusted. And whatever people might say, it's not *that* much slower either. Not so that you'd sacrifice Bitcoin's security and credibility anyway.

In addition, it's not Bitcoin that has the fee issue at the moment, it's Ethereum, because they are trying to be so many things to so many people. More on Ethereum as we go through the book. But running all the Dapps (decentralised apps) and smart contracting on their EVM

(Ethereum Virtual Machine), as well as the currency itself, is straining the Ethereum blockchain at the moment. Mind you, it has historically has been a little bit on and off (see investing tips). But, to be fair, they are in pole position at the cutting edge of a brand-new transformative technology. So, yeah. Hopefully Ethereum 2.0 will change all that, because they've worked extremely hard on it. But scaling up smart contracts on a blockchain is not as easy as some would have you believe, and requires massive computing power. Ethereum really is a huge deal in decentralised computing, finance, and a lot of other benefitting fields, so I hope they succeed in expanding their capabilities. Sorry, Bitcoin, we were talking about you.

If the public at large accept that Bitcoin is money, whether they sit on it, use it every day, or trade it; doesn't matter. From where I'm sitting, a healthy minority already has declared it to be money. Surely it's perfect? Especially if money can also be beads, gold, goats, carved bits of stone, or even pretty printed bits of paper. Imagine that. Who the hell would swap a perfectly good goat for a few bits of paper. They must be mad.

Money exchange, up until Bitcoin, had required the banks and payment providers to build a considerable series of connections, relationships, physical offices, staff, marketing budgets, etc., on and on. This obviously costs a great deal of money as it simultaneously relies on a lot of expensive people and resources across many borders and institutions. And, unavoidably, all that is factored-in to every single thing we buy today. VISA charges merchants 2 or 3 per cent for starters. Then there are business bank charges, 1% to bank cash, factoring (borrowing against) debt to help cashflow. That's not a lot, but it's certainly an added bonus and only a handful of the things Bitcoin improves. All transactions can now completely sidestep this old-fashioned labyrinth - me to you, and nothing in between.

Settlement is near-instant, taking place in less than an hour, down to even seconds. The cost to fulfil these transactions is minimal, whether transferring a few dollars' worth or far more. Already there have been cross border payments of $200 million worth that were instant and cost less than a dollar to complete - securely and virtually instantly. Furthermore, once the Bitcoin, or perhaps just a couple of hundred Satoshis, is in your electronic wallet, the transaction is impossible to reverse. So you can be confident that the money is yours. Yes, it really is money. Even PayPal accept it now, not before time, allowing you to convert it on-the-spot into whatever currency the merchant requires, Crypto or fiat. And you can still swap it for a cow if you really really want to.

4. WHAT IS BLOCKCHAIN AND DISTRIBUTED LEDGER?

"The ledger, the distributed database – it's called a Blockchain – is held in the cloud by all parties involved. It can't be broken by any of them. Its cryptography is too strong. You would have to compromise the entire network to take over Bitcoin."
Naval Ravikant, co-founder AngelList

Bitcoin, and most cryptocurrencies that came after it, employs a brand-new technology called Blockchain. In simple terms, it is just an accounting ledger of all transactions ever to have been completed by every person ever to have used Bitcoin. Think of it as a giant filing cabinet. Each file, in each drawer, contains transaction details for a certain period, which in the case of Bitcoin is roughly every ten minutes and 500 transactions worth. The files, one after another, are placed sequentially in a drawer and kept forever. Now think of each file as a 'block' and link these blocks sequentially together in a physical chain - or Blockchain. The entire filing cabinet is the Blockchain. The same technique can be used for any number of applications that require a secure record of any kind of transaction or data to be made. It's the ultimate secure and decentralised solution to many problems.

Cryptographic techniques are used to verify and link these transactions using what is called a 'Hash Function'. Data from the previous block is computationally hashed together (or mixed) with the new block, using cryptographic methods. These, in turn, are hashed with the block before that, and so on, so that it cannot be undone. The algorithms contain an impossible-to-unravel computation of long alphanumeric sequences combined with public and private 'keys'. The technique is called public and private key cryptography. A Bitcoin owner holds an electronic or printed paper 'wallet' which has both a public key and private key. The latter proves ownership, in a way like a password, since the Bitcoin owner keeps it secret and it cannot be unravelled from the other data in the hash. The public key can be handed out for others to pay into, similar to you giving me your bank account number. As long as the private key is kept secret, the Cryptocurrency is safe and only ever accessible by that one person. A private key is a random 256-bit number, equating to 64 hexadecimal characters in a row when written down. So it would take approximately 0.65 billion billion years to crack with existing computing technology. In terms of the number of 'tries', that's a 1 followed by 77 zeros (2^256)! Oh, what the heck, let's write that in full for maximum effect - 100,000,000,000,000,000,000,000,000,000,000,000,000,000,000,000,000,000,000,000,000,000,000,000,000,000,000.

So it's safe then, just as long as you keep that private key safe! We'll get to how to secure this safely later in the book. But here comes the clever bit that we alluded to in the last chapter. Identical copies of the entire ledger are contained in thousands of different computers all around the world so that there is no single point where the data is stored. Hence no single attack vector. Any change in the Blockchain needs to be verified by other nodes on the network and be present on all copies worldwide. This makes it impossible to hack or change, as you cannot hack all of them at once. You might be able to change one or two versions of the data, but you won't be able to change them all – almost 100,000 nodes now, in the case of Bitcoin.
This is called a *distributed ledger*, and it runs on a decentralised network. Decentralisation is the buzzword, the key to everything, and it underpins Bitcoin's technology and most of the blockchain movement. It is that which gives it its trust-less and uncompromised properties. Banks have their own way of storing databases of transactions. However, this is usually highly centralised, in a specific building or on one particular single set of servers, entirely controlled by only a few people. This makes it prone to hacking, with a much lower attack vector of, at most, a few machines. It also gives a single institution complete control of your assets and costs, not to mention forcing you to use dinosaur money.

Bitcoin, by comparison, is controlled by tens of thousands of people. It is worth noting here that not all cryptocurrencies are decentralised like this. In fact, a lot are owned and controlled by a corporation or single entity. Bitcoin, with its anonymous and open source (free to all) code, is different. As such, it cannot be stopped by any government, law or organisation, unless the entire internet was shut down. It is out there and out there to stay. Plus, the biggest Blockchain is generally the safest, because of the enormous amount of data you would need to unravel to pick it apart. This, however, does come with a bit of an Achilles heel.

5. WHAT IS MINING?

"The credit/debit card transaction system is antiquated, expensive, and inefficient. There are over nine steps to complete a transaction from the time a customer swipes their card to payment processing, settlement, and when the merchant finally gets paid. Every step along the way costs both the consumer and the vendor in additional fees."
Perianne Boring, founder DigitalChamber.org

All of this requires enormous amounts of computing power, even though blockchain technology tries to allow anyone with the resources to 'mine' Bitcoin or other cryptocurrencies. "Heigh-ho, heigh-ho, it's off to work we go"! No, not that kind. This is our second misnomer and can be a bit confusing. Miners are not really *mining* anything, rather they are confirming transactions on the network and adding them to the Blockchain. In return for this, they are automatically rewarded with free Cryptocurrency by the Bitcoin software. They don't really 'mine' it as such. Still, it's a reasonably good comparison to physically mining gold, in that both require work, effort and rarity to define their value. Having said that, Bitcoin nor gold can be automatically guaranteed their value just because the work has already been done. Proof-of-work does not automatically and exclusively guarantee proof-of-success. Only once the rocks, or the numbers, have been crunched, can the market get to decide whether the formula provides value. It's the same with all forms of asset, past, present, or future. Thankfully, the market has decided that Bitcoin does have value. *Significant* value at that, and a real future. Remember, it has been around 12 years after all. All manner of naysayers have tried to discredit it, and Bitcoin just brushes them off. This is not a flash in the pan. It's not even a 'tech-bubble' any more. Bitcoin has proved itself to be a contender.

It really helps to understand the mining process correctly, which is a little trickier to fully grasp right off-the-bat. Because, well, it genuinely seems a bit bonkers at first. But, rest assured, there are reasons for everything that Satoshi has done. Suppose we remember the work element of centuries-old money systems like the Rai stone or gold. The same principle applies to Bitcoin. Their value is determined partly because of the sheer amount of work that has gone in to hew the stone or dig up the gold. In the same way, Bitcoin is deliberately difficult to 'mine' because the code forces miners to complete challenging mathematical problems to gain a chance of writing the next block to the Blockchain. This difficulty is intentional, giving it an ever-increasing value and helping to keep the network robust (safe). Not just anybody can do it because it takes serious resources, but there are many mining collectives made up of thousands of public individuals' computers, called mining pools. A consensus is reached among the group of miners, and the first person or pool to complete the task correctly is rewarded in Crypto. Nobody knows who that is until several miners have effectively come up with the same answer and thus the network, as a whole, has sufficiently verified all the transactions in the block. Effectively everyone is working together towards the same end. That means that the block is checked multiple times before it gets added to the Blockchain. In the case of Bitcoin, each block always takes ten minutes to solve. To use our earlier analogy, we are putting a file in the filing cabinet (Blockchain) every ten minutes. The difficulty of the computational task is changed regularly, according to demand, to achieve that. This is another brilliant subtlety, introduced by Bitcoin. Bitcoin is always running the numbers and evolving accordingly, all by itself. Miners are rewarded in newly minted Bitcoin that the code distributes with each completed block. The block-reward since May 2020 has been 6.25 coins per block, which is a considerable amount. The code cleverly alters the scarcity of Bitcoin, and computational difficulty, according to demand and worldwide mining capacity. It will take until the year 2040 to mine the last 2.5 million or so Bitcoins. The first 18.5 million or so have already been mined in the first twelve years. As part of the economic/technology rules of Bitcoin, this reward halves approximately every four years, or every 210,000 blocks. From 50 Bitcoins per block in 2009 halving three times to 6.25 in 2020. This makes the coins in circulation scarcer, and thus, the theory goes, more valuable. This process is called 'the Halving' or 'Halvening', and many cryptocurrencies operate in the same way. Rewards are different for other coins, and in fact, since October 2020, Ethereum miners now receive more in fees (gas) than they do in block rewards. This is due to the vast number of smart contracts running on their Blockchain, which has recently pushed prices sky-high. Horses for courses though, Bitcoin just sticks to what it's good at. Money. More on Smart Contracts and Ethereum in chapter 8.

One significant factor which is critical to the value is that the code automatically adjusts the difficulty of mining according to demand and market value. So, at times, it takes less effort than at others, depending on how many people are trying to solve it, and what the demands on the system are. The beautiful code brings solid economic theory at every turn, while simultaneously being one of the most innovative pieces of tech in our lifetime. There are others, don't get me wrong, like DNA editing or the internet itself. But Bitcoin is right up there.

Thus the Bitcoin blockchain is super secure, and prevents problems like 'Double Spend', where the owner of an electronic currency spends it twice. The robust and decentralised mining network verifies that it can only ever be spent once. Once it's hashed in a block, it can't be retracted or changed - ever. In fact it's not Bitcoin you have to worry about getting hacked, it's you, or your email, or a wallet or a third party company or exchange you're using. And anything that's sitting on top of the Bitcoin blockchain itself. You still need to take care of those basics, all your passwords and 2FA (2-factor authentication), and always be on the lookout for phishing or worse.

As I have said, Bitcoin does have an Achilles heel. Power. The entire system of servers worldwide was, by late spring 2020, using an astonishing 7 gigawatts of electricity, or 64-terawatt hours (TWh) of power annually, twenty times that of Facebook's servers (5.1 TWh in 2019). That's as much as several countries' total consumption - for example, Portugal, Switzerland, Chile, Kuwait or Ireland.

Horrific as that sounds, that's not the whole story. Most people don't realise how much the internet itself uses, with giant server farms all over the world now. It's no co-incidence that many of these are neighbours of some of the world's largest fossil fuel power plants. Bitcoin represents 'only' around 1000th of the total energy used by the internet as a whole. In fact around 62 trillion spam messages are sent every year, requiring the use of 33bn kilowatt hours (KWh) of electricity and causing around 20 million tonnes of CO2e per year. Not a lot of people know that.

Importantly, in reality, much of this comes from renewable energy sources, such as geothermal in Iceland, or excess capacity of hydroelectric power in countries like China. Much of the Chinese power is already excess to requirements, especially in the rainy season, and it has about the cheapest electricity in the world at the moment.

Add to that the fact that to run any payments system like a bank requires physical buildings, entire skyscrapers in major cities, staff driving to work every day and other colossal running costs. Not to mention their own server costs. It starts to make a bit more sense. Additionally, the likely progression is that technology will advance quickly enough so that the hardware will become faster more and more energy-efficient as time goes on. Like renewable energy itself, there are challenges, but the future is undoubtedly electronic.

6. WHO'S IN CHARGE?

"Governments are good at cutting off the heads of centrally controlled networks like Napster, but pure P2P networks like Gnutella and Tor seem to be holding their own."
Satoshi Nakamoto

The short answer is nobody is in charge. And all of us are.

To keep the flag flying, Bitcoin is under constant development and supervision, while still maintaining decentralisation. No one person or organisation gets to decide the rules. This really is the key to Bitcoin's invulnerability. Most of the essential rules governing Bitcoin were inherited from Satoshi Nakamoto, and have stayed the same fundamentally. Still, there have been many times when the code base has needed updating or changing, as with any software. This is no easy feat since in a decentralised, anonymous and open source space, any change, however minor, has to reach consensus in the network of miners, nodes, users, and Bitcoin holders. That's a good thing. There is nothing to stop anyone releasing their own version, as the code base is open source and always will be. This means that it can be used by anyone and updated or changed. Many 'Altcoins' have done just that, changing little but the name. But that's not necessarily going to result in a decentralised coin with community consensus. And unless it's agreed by the community, it isn't going to be Bitcoin either. They call it the 'wisdom of the crowd' for a reason. It does seem to work.

Fortunately, Bitcoin is very robust and has a large number of people keeping it sharp. Much of this is paid for by members of the community with an interest in seeing it succeed, or given as a labour of love. Consequently, Bitcoin is in great shape as a result. Many other cryptocurrencies, or altcoins, have little or no dev work going on, and this is generally a vital sign as to whether they have a future or not.

The Governance process starts with the 'Bitcoin Core' development team, originally just four people, which now has over 300 contributors variously working on BTC alone. Initially led by Gavin Andresen, the person to whom Satoshi Nakamoto handed the responsibility before disappearing forever, it's now headed up by Wladimir J. van der Laan. At the same time, Gavin concentrates on the strategic development of the technology. No single person can simply change the code, though, without consensus. Because the code is open source, there is nothing to stop more and more versions of Bitcoin coming out, and this has happened. But it is up to us, the user, to decide which one we use. The original, Bitcoin Core (BTC), has always been my choice so far.

Core devs can suggest alterations or additions to the code, whether syntax, security or more significant changes. When a researcher has discovered a solution to a problem, they share this either with the bitcoin-dev mailing list, or via a formal white paper. This is called a Bitcoin Improvement Proposal or BIP. For example, BIP39 proposed that users could use a mnemonic key-phrase of English-language words to remember the long private keys. This democratic collaboration is standard in the development of open-source projects. In fact, BIP is modelled on the programming language Python, with its 'Python Enhancement Proposal' (PEP). Most of Bitcoin's BIPs are concerned with formatting or transaction data to gradually improve upon what Satoshi started with.

Rest assured, you're not likely to see a fundamental change in the code that, say, increased the number of coins from 21 million to 221 million. This is in nobody's interest and would be impossible to gain consensus on. When a proposal is made, if it receives a favourable peer review, it can become part of the code. This is called a 'soft-fork' and is backwards compatible with the software, meaning it becomes part of the code. If not, the proposer can release his or her own version of the Bitcoin software with their personal changes. This is not difficult, and they, or a collection of people might start using it. Still, it's no longer BTC, or backwards compatible, so transactions cannot be completed on the original BTC blockchain anymore. Instead, this so-called 'hard-fork' will go on by another name...Bitcoin Cash BCH, Bitcoin Gold BTG, Bitcoin SV (Satoshi Vision) BSV or Bitcoin-Whatever-Next. They're not the same, despite some of the confusing claims made, but each has its own aims, and it is up to the free market whether or not they are taking the right path.

A BIP can be approved without a 100% consensus. It's the nodes who choose whether to adopt it or not. There's no reason both branches of the fork can't continue to be used. But chances are, unless there's a compelling reason not to upgrade, the old branch will fall into disuse. This is an excellent way of managing development democratically, and this is one of the beautiful things about open source code, which is free for all, and combined with the strengths of a distributed network.

Hard forks in the code usually happen when there are disagreements between community members who have argued for one set of rules over another. In the case of Bitcoin, as I say this has led to several hard-forks (versions) of the coin. Perhaps the most famous of them is Bitcoin Cash. If a certain number of users, nodes and miners (say 80%) want to take a different approach with the code, they can vote to spawn a second chain out of the first, or hard fork. As we've said, a soft fork is more of an update of current code and features, completed by consensus. So it was that in 2017, Bitcoin Cash evangelists, led by Roger Ver, famously called Bitcoin Jesus, voted to fork into a new coin to increase the number of possible transactions. This left behind the original Bitcoin blockchain and created another with the same 21 million total. All original Bitcoin holders were given one BCH for each BTC they owned. The two chains then continued independently of one another. It's worth noting that Mr Ver owns the domain name bitcoin.com and they claim Bitcoin Cash BCH to be the 'real Bitcoin'. This is not true. Bitcoin, BTC, is Bitcoin, a huge and secure blockchain with a far greater market penetration, user base and trust. Accordingly, it's still the big fish - the Amazon or Google of the Cryptocurrency world. But that doesn't mean to say that Bitcoin Cash is without merit. A year later, Bitcoin Cash itself forked again, and BitcoinSV was created, standing for Satoshi Vision. This time it was self-proclaimed 'Real Satoshi', Craig

Wright, an Australian computer scientist, leading the charge. His claim to be Nakamoto was quickly disproven in court, by the way. Currently, with no proof of who Satoshi is, anyone can use the name Bitcoin, as it is impossible to enforce a trademark. So don't be surprised if there are yet more versions of Bitcoin. And more companies using the *word* Bitcoin. Who knows, it's not entirely inconceivable that this might one day change though. Will the real Satoshi Nakamoto please stand up; I repeat, will the real Satoshi Nakamoto please stand up?

In July 2015, the Ethereum blockchain was hacked, resulting in the loss of $64 million in Ether. The creators and network decided to reverse the transaction by hard forking the coin into what we now know as Ethereum ETH. The old coin, this time primarily left behind, became known as Ether Classic ETC. This was a hugely controversial decision because one of the main points of a distributed ledger is that it cannot be changed or undone. It's a cardinal sin in the blockchain world, and unlikely ever to happen to Bitcoin. In theory, though, it could if there was an overall consensus. Luckily there is far too much resistance to this these days, and miners, nodes and the community at large, for the most part, agree.

In 2012 a new organisation called the Bitcoin Foundation was formed, which intended to ensure proper oversight. This was funded and led by projects in the space that rely on Bitcoin. They all want to see its continued success. Various crypto and blockchain luminaries have been elected to the board over the years, and this changes reasonably regularly.

The board also (but not exclusively) makes recommendations on Bitcoin standards, protects the network and promotes it to an ever-wider audience. In case you were still in any doubt, there are a lot of talented people working on Bitcoin, many of whom have bet the farm, and that's another reason that it's here to stay.

7. 10 USES FOR BLOCKCHAIN AND CRYPTOCURRENCY

"In fact, Blockchain has the potential to fundamentally change how we share information, buy and sell things, interact with government, prove our identity, and even verify the authenticity of everything – from the food we eat, to the medicine we take, to who we say we are"
Julie Sweet, CEO Accenture

While money is an excellent application for a decentralised blockchain, possibly the best, there are many other use cases too. It's not the answer to everything, but if you really need to trust the data and not rely on any single authority to do that, you can see how it might revolutionise much of what we compute today.

If we think of a blockchain as an immutable, secure method for storing information and conducting business without any need for a third party, the opportunities are extensive. That said, Blockchain really isn't the solution to all the world's problems, as some would have you believe. Where a database is required, it need not necessarily be on a secure blockchain, depending on the application. Sometimes a single server is enough. But with a blockchain doing the work or executing 'smart contracts' for you, there can be a considerable saving of time and admin. Not to mention iron-clad security like we have never seen before. All we need to do is trust the code, and code is law. Here are just a few of the applications being explored by new start-ups and existing companies as we speak.

Currency - Bitcoin began as a peer-to-peer (P2P) electronic cash system. Anyone can hold bitcoin and pay anyone without a middle-man. Examples: Bitcoin, Litecoin, Monero.

Payment Infrastructure - You can use Bitcoin/Altcoins to send money around the world. Merchants can accept coin payments. Uses cases include merchant processing and remittances. Examples: BitPay, Abra, CryptoPay, Ripple XRP (used by over 100 banks) and now PayPal.

Digital Assets - A blockchain can be used to create digital assets such as stocks, bonds, land titles, or perhaps frequent flyer miles. Examples: Swiss Stock Exchange SIX, NASDAQ, Openchain.

Identity - Companies will start to offer blockchain ID's that can be used to sign into apps and web sites, digitally sign documents, vote etc. Because it would use a blockchain, where we know the information can be trusted, this finally means that your data will be safe, used only for purpose, and won't be sold on. This will become the standard. Examples: Blockchain Technologies, Consensys, Cardano (ADA), Keybase, Zug ID, and many more to come.

Verifiable Data - Create a verifiable record of any data, file, or business process on the Blockchain. Examples: HashedHealth, Tierion, Proof of Existence, Factom

Smart Contracts - Software programs that live on the Blockchain and execute without the possibility of third-party interference. Examples: Ethereum, NEM, NEO, Hyperledger and even Bitcoin.

ICO – Initial Coin Offering. The 'bigger-than-an-IPO' fundraising method - offering tokens currently bought through smart contracts to raise development funds in the tens of millions (with little regulation and few conditions attached to the funding). Now mainly facilitated by Ethereum's smart contracts platform. See the next chapter.

Monitoring Supply Chains - By removing paper-based trails and replacing them with an immutable blockchain, companies can keep track of their supply chains. They can verify the authenticity and origin of a product, and prove provenance as they move through the supply chain. Examples: Walmart, Maersk Shipping, British Airways, UPS.

Digital Voting - Blockchain has the capability to secure voting in a way that has never been achieved before. Especially in the wake of

Covid-19. Its immutability ensures no fraud and has the potential to conduct an election in real-time and without the massive effort that it currently takes. Examples: Kaspersky, Agora, Polys.

Copyright and royalty protection - Blockchain has the potential to pay rights holders (musicians, say) directly for their content without needing to go through a middle-man. Payments can be in real-time and without delay. And users can know exactly where their money has gone. Examples: Steam, Choon, Musicoin, Mycelia.

8. TOKEN FEVER - SMART CONTRACTS & THE ICO MONEY-MACHINE

"Listen. Take the best. Leave the rest."
Richard Branson

Bitcoin may be the first and still Daddy of all cryptocurrencies, but it's definitely not alone. I'm certainly a believer or 'Bitcoin Maximalist' as it's called. However, incredibly, there are 5000+ other 'tokens' out there, all of them born after Bitcoin. There might be as many as 7,000. The vast majority of these are in the new world of Decentralised Finance (DeFi), which we talk about a bit more in the final chapter. This brave new world is a vast minefield of success stories, failures and, inevitably, straight-up cons. Almost all of them have some grounding in the original and current Bitcoin codebase which, being open-source, is viewable and useable by anyone. Its decentralised, distributed nature ensures that the code remains open to inspection always. At its simplest level, anyone with a basic coding knowledge can take that code, change the names and headers and effectively launch a new coin. Of course, you need people to use and buy the coin, and miners to mine it, so those without a clear use case have failed to take hold, even if they initially gained some support.

By virtue of Bitcoin being the first, all these other coins are called Altcoins. Many have gained spectacular success too, and a few even have slightly different ambitions.

Bitcoin, while initially aimed as being a day-to-day payment system, has somewhat become more of a store of value, like digital gold. It's just as difficult to mine, just like gold is. Gold requires huge plant machinery to dig and crush rocks at a rate of about 2 to 90 tons of stone for a single ounce. Once you've found where to dig in the first place, of course. Similarly, Bitcoin, as we have discovered, uses a tremendous amount of computing power and electricity to achieve the same use case. It's out of that work to value ratio, economic principles, scarcity, and of course, the outstandingly good tech that it has become valuable. Bitcoin has the added advantage of being much safer and far more fungible. That is to say, usable on the spot. You don't have to go to a vault and unlock it, for one thing. Plus we don't know how much gold is out there. If Mr Branson, Musk or Bezos somehow managed to send an asteroid back to us, it may contain more precious metals than we have here on earth. It's not such a crazy thought either. A recent Hubble asteroid discovery '16 Psyche' contains about $10,000 quadrillion worth of metals. Bring that back, and the metal it carries will then only have industrial manufacturing value. Gold could become worthless in theory. Imagine if that actually happened one day. There will only ever be 21 million Bitcoin though.

In October 2011, while Bitcoin was still gaining traction, a talented coder and ex-Google employee called Charlie Lee created a variant of Bitcoin called Litecoin. It was designed to be faster and cheaper to transact with than Bitcoin and differed only slightly to achieve that. It's also a deflationary coin like Bitcoin so, as such, it too has a finite supply. Litecoin has a maximum number of 84 million coins, which is four times that of Bitcoin. And it mines a block every 2.5 minutes; a quarter of the time to mine a Bitcoin block. Like Bitcoin, it uses a 'proof-of-work' algorithm, which is to say that it stores a proof of all work (transactions) or changes on its Blockchain. Despite being virtually a copy of Bitcoin, it has a real use case (speed and transaction costs), and is completely decentralised and open source. It therefore remains one of the early (and existing) success stories.

Not all cryptocurrencies employ the same proof-of-work technique. Others, called proof-of-stake, rely on a number of nodes through which owners always hold coins to participate. This 'staking' gives the owner of the node regular dividends too. However, it is questionable whether this is strictly legal in most jurisdictions due to complex securities legislation. This is far more energy-efficient than proof-of-work, because it requires only consensus from a comparatively small number of participants or stakeholders. Theoretically, this should still be secure, but it does open the doors to potentially cede more of that decentralised control to just a handful of people. Plus, any individual or committee control over a network presents a vulnerability that, in the future, governments or outside forces could use to control or shut down a coin. Nobody owns or controls a Proof Of Work (POW) coin like Bitcoin, so it can't be stopped. We are talking about money here, which is not a frivolous subject, and money will go where it's safest. In my opinion, there is *no way* the wealth of the world will be put in the hands of *any* POS chain and its handful of enthusiastic stakeholders right now. Maybe the concept will develop, but we'll have to see.

If the name of the game is decentralised, untouchable and secure, then a massive energy-inefficient blockchain does the job very well, like it or not. Conversely, and to be balanced about it, Bitcoin itself is, in theory at least, open to potential centralisation if all the miners were concentrated in the same place. Some people worry about the concentration of Chinese miners who, with their cheap electricity, now control over 60% of the network. But this is divided amongst thousands of competing miners. Own 51% of the network in one place and you can undo the very Blockchain itself with a '51% attack', and this has happened with some of the smaller chains. This is where you have superior computing capacity and become over 51% of the chain's total 'Hash rate'. This, as you can imagine, is costly. Let's also not forget that, if your motivation as an attacker is money-oriented, you'd be shooting yourself in the foot to attack any blockchain. It could wipe out all confidence and hence the value attached to it. Plus, to achieve this on a huge and valuable blockchain like Bitcoin would require enormously expensive computing power to compete with the miners already there. Currently, a sustained attack on Bitcoin would cost around 21 million dollars a day. Ethereum costs around a tenth of that. All of these things change with time. More and more ideas are being brought to the fore as the industry, and the codebase matures. 51% attacks are now highly unlikely. But, theoretically at least, it's a 'thing'.

At the end of 2013, the co-founder of Bitcoin Magazine, Vitalik Buterin, proposed a brand-new idea. Vitalik, a Russian-Canadian programmer used decentralised blockchain technology to create the 'Ethereum Virtual Machine (EVM)', and with it a corresponding currency called Ethereum. For the next two years, he and three other co-founders put together one of the single most important developments in the history of financial technology (Fintech). Easily as important as Bitcoin. Ethereum allowed for simple decentralised apps (Dapps) to be written and executed on the network. Ethereum charged a small 'Gas' fee in Ether (their coin) for each instruction or transaction to keep the system unclogged and functioning. With this powerful tool, users could now issue their own crypto tokens and blockchains using so-called smart contracts. These enabled fairly straightforward tasks to be completed without interference from anyone, in a decentralised manner, without having to rely on trusting a third party. So now you could write a handful of lines of script to perform a task subject to a set of circumstances. For example, pay person A 10 ETH tokens if they complete task B. The contracts remain open until executed on the Ethereum Dapp (decentralised app). They can't be altered or interfered with by any third party.

This, in turn, gave way for the rise and rise of the phenomenon called the ICO, or Initial Coin Offering. Now people could issue a new coin, let's say Andrew-Coin, on the Ethereum network. They can use their protocols, and raise money through an ICO by selling the tokens to the general public. These are usually in exchange for Ethereum or Bitcoin, and locked in a smart contract. ICO takes its name from the IPO, or Initial Public Offering, used all over the world to raise money for new or existing businesses by listing on the stock exchange. However, the ICO didn't bother with all of those pesky rules and regulations, of course not. At the time, the ICO essentially became a free for all fund-raising method with very few barriers and even less oversight. This is fantastic for innovation and genuine development, however not so much for dealing with scammers and fake projects. Accordingly, governments around the world are now, years later, starting to take legal action against some of the bad actors, and some who have blatantly disregarded the so-called 'rules'. Let's be clear, this is not Ethereum's fault or doing, just for providing the tools. Or its intention either. Even the US government has no problem with Ethereum per se. But, while some people love giving the middle finger to government, it's not okay that, in the wake of little to no regulation, a lot of ordinary people lost their money as a result. The vast majority of cryptocurrency tokens out there are based on the Ethereum network as what's called ERC20 tokens (and others) based on the Ethereum token itself. Investors pledged Ethereum in a smart contract sale, which could last anything from a few minutes to several weeks.

These are some of the success stories. Blockchain Capital; $10 million raised in 6 hours. Bancor; $152 million raised in 3 hours. Brave (web browser); $35 million raised in 30 seconds. Tezos; $232 million with $160 million of it raised within the first 32 hours. Then, into the big leagues, the world's biggest (and now deemed illegal) was for Telegram, the messaging app. They raised a whopping $1.7 billion only to be forced to give back 70%, plus an easily-afforded $18.5m civil penalty.

Ethereum itself brought in $18 million with its own ICO back in 2014. First movers were lucky enough to buy at just 40 cents. This climbed to $14 per coin in 2016 and was hovering around the $200 to $300 mark for most of 2020. It briefly hit an all-time bubble-high of $1,400 in 2018 along with most of the market, but that was short-lived. These days it does seem to be growing more organically, as does Bitcoin. This brings confidence to the space, which is actually good news.

By 2017 $10 billion was being raised annually, which is more than all IPO's put together on regular stock exchanges. In 2018 $11.4 billion flowed in. But by 2019, with increasing regulatory pressure, this figure had dropped to $317 million. ICO's still exist but have to be conducted more in line with a regular share offering, with all the associated documentation and compliance of Anti Money Laundering rules (AML). They are, after all, mostly de-facto Securities Offerings, and as such subject to strict regulations to protect consumers. This is not necessarily a bad thing. It's worth noting that Ethereum can be particularly volatile in price at times of ICO activity. Once they're conducted, and the Ether has been raised, the recipient company starts to use the funds immediately and is thus selling onto the market and driving the price down. Similarly, when ICO investors are buying, the price goes up.

There are now over 5000 cryptocurrencies, but *at least half* of these are dead coins or scams. Look for a real product, exchange listings and developer engagement, and you can soon see which. Most were birthed, pumped briefly to a once-only 'all-time high' price, never to be seen again. Check out coinopsy.com for some excellent analysis.

Factors affecting whether it's a scam or not are generally pretty obvious; "Oh look at this innovative, exclusive way to make shed loads of money with zero product or effort". So if you don't understand the white paper, no shame, a fair amount are nonsense anyway. Or worse, they contain plagiarism of other people's bullshit. This is surprisingly common, yet still people hand their money over. Look for the obvious stuff: like spelling mistakes, check whether the website is https, does it promise abnormally high returns (in itself a clear legal definition of a Security offering), is there a legitimate community, are the owners' identities obscured or even faked, are there claims to have celebrity endorsements, is the CEO a pet dog or a clip-art CEO...well you get the picture. To be fair, these companies aren't incredibly bright about it.

A new fundraising method called IEO's is also now gaining popularity. These 'Initial Exchange Offerings' are conducted on a cryptocurrency exchange. They are supposed to have thoroughly evaluated the offering, with investor checks as standard to stem the flow of scams, money laundering and terrorist financing. Note that these too can be classified as Securities retrospectively. So, unless the IEO has been conducted legally, it can be frozen by the authorities. Where the exchange is based, whether it's legal, and what laws apply, as we see in chapter 12, are critical factors.

Many people have seen gains by a factor of thousands of times their initial investment, and of course, many more have lost money due to pump and dump schemes along the way. Common sense rules apply here just as much as anywhere else. Clichés abound, but they are no less important. 'A fool and his money are easily parted' and 'If it seems too good to be true, it probably is'. If there is one piece of advice here, it's that you never invest until you've done your research and are confident you understand where the money is going. All the ICOs choose a lot of similar technical terminology, some of it even straight-up plagiarised (nicked) from each other. If you feel yourself falling into the trap of thinking they're smarter than you and are the new geniuses, don't get caught up. Bluntly, if you don't understand it fully, don't touch until you do.

Some companies who have either been involved in selling and issuing ICO tokens are being sued or facing government prosecution for trading unregistered securities, or other misdemeanours. These include Bitfinex, Binance, BitMEX, the Tron Foundation, Block.One and many more. Before you buy an existing token or a new one, you must be sure that it passes these rules. The Securities and Exchange Commission in the US has already been taking legal action against ICO's for failing to complete KYC or 'know your customer'. As an investor, if you haven't been asked who you are and where you got your money, then chances are you're on shaky ground. It might take the authorities time to catch up to your particular coin, but there's every chance of it eventually getting shut down.

On the other hand, decentralised issuance of tokens is a fantastic way for new businesses to raise funds. Just because they have chosen to do an ICO or similar method, it doesn't make them dishonest. It avoids prohibitively costly compliance and a lengthy path to market, or at least has the opportunity of making it more accessible, so the market will definitely evolve.

Cryptocurrencies or tokens can be divided into three groups - Utility tokens, Payment tokens and Security tokens. These titles have come about mostly because of regulatory pressures, seeing governments around the world clamp down hard on what they see as potentially illegal securities issuance, in their eyes at least. To date, issuers of cryptocurrencies have been able to do so without any oversight. At the same time, regular stock issuance is subject to very extreme scrutiny. Like it or not, this is starting to affect the way the industry works.

Tokens are seen very much as investment instruments, like stocks and shares, and if we are honest, a lot of them really are. This was not Satoshi's original vision of utility, but a lot of people buy them simply to speculate, and a free market with hundreds of trading exchanges sets the price. It is the job of government authorities to protect its public investors from the total loss of their investment, so you can expect them to attempt to do that from now on. I will always maintain that it's not always a bad thing. Many jurisdictions, led by Switzerland, in Zug Canton (Crypto Valley), have designed a framework where innovation can be tested in what's called a 'Sandbox' environment. So put down that shiny technical-sounding prospectus you might be reading, don't invest if it doesn't make sense. Don't invest if the token's legality is not clear. But do your homework correctly, and don't kid yourself. There is big money to be made in crypto speculation: both short term profits and long-term return.

Utility tokens - These exist to serve some sort of function, like for example paying fees on an exchange or providing a guarantee to use of a network's products or services

Payment tokens - a token that is used primarily for paying for goods and services, as if it is money. Bitcoin, Litecoin and Ethereum can be included in this category.

Security tokens - any token that is issued with the expectancy of a return on investment (ROI) or dividend and interest payments, is classed as a full Security under securities laws. So they must adhere to the same rules and disclosure as any IPO or regular share sale. It is also these laws that could stop a lot of DeFi staking and earning projects. We get to these in our final chapter.

Importantly, it's worth noting that a token might sit in two or all three groups at once. In a recent tightening of rules, the international Financial Action Task Force (FATF) has recommended to governments around the world that *all* tokens are to be classified as Securities in the future. Not all countries agree, even though they are supposed to fall in line, so this has not yet gained widespread acceptance.

Currently these tokens also don't necessarily provide any right to ownership or equity in the company, unless explicitly stated, even if it's been classified a security. Further, unless the ICO provides guarantees for what the money will be used for, you will not have any rights here either. The issuer can do whatever they like with the money, and a lot have done just that, as you can imagine. Of course, it is not in the interests of most to kill their own coin, so this abuse is rare or under the radar. Again, research research research until you're sure. You can't go far wrong typing NAME and SCAM into Google to see what comes up. Even though it's a totally new asset class, it's wise to always be a 'fundamental' investor. Ensure there is a real team with a real use case (with actual usage), not to mention a genuine product behind the hype.

9. TRADING CRYPTOCURRENCIES - 29 ESSENTIAL FACTORS AFFECTING PRICE

"I don't throw darts at a board. I bet on sure things. Read Sun Tzu, The Art of War. Every battle is won before it is ever fought."
Gordon Gekko in the film Wall Street, 1987

The film Wall Street came out in 1987, an almost prophetic prediction of the stock market crash on Oct 19th of that year, and everything that's wrong with the system. If you're familiar with the film, you'll know that Michael Douglas' dispassionate character was the king of Wall Street... until, er, he wasn't. Believe you're an investing genius, and the rules don't apply to you, and there will always be someone waiting to take your money, or in GG's case lock you up. Plus, it's easy to feel like you've got it nailed in a bull market that's significantly on the rise. *My God, I might actually be Gordon Gekko, I'm so good.*

The reality is that there are a considerable number of factors affecting the rise and fall of crypto prices which are different to all other investments. It is not the same as charting Forex or stock prices, for which there is still a far higher daily volume. This means that far and away, the main factor affecting prices of cryptocurrencies is what the major players are up to. Suppose you're a 'whale' and can dump - say - two hundred million dollars of Bitcoin into the market. In that case, this is going to substantially affect the price (downwards). Similarly, a significant buy-in would raise the market price. This is not nearly as acute in Foreign exchange capital markets (Forex), where around 5 trillion dollars are traded daily. It's almost impossible to control the price as a result. Bitcoin might see $10 billion worth in volume, or more, traded back and forth in a day, with bitcoins changing hands multiple times. Still, it's far far easier to manipulate with this 'relatively' low number.

Smaller coins with much smaller daily trading volumes and market cap can be manipulated by far less, even a few tens of thousands of dollars and a couple of pieces of fake news. You can have all the charts in the world, follow the news daily, as I do, but nothing can predict who will buy when unless you actually know that person. So tread carefully. Thankfully the soon-to-fail economies of the world have nothing to do with Bitcoin or Crypto. If anything, it should be a safe haven when leveraged debt-based economies are falling apart. There follows a list of a few factors affecting the price that you should be looking out for. Oh, and if you haven't read it already, The Art of War, by 5th-century Chinese general and philosopher, Sun Tzu, really is an excellent little book. So as you peruse the rest of this chapter, here's another of his gems. "*The quality of decision is like the well-timed swoop of a falcon which enables it to strike and destroy its victim*".

• Technical trading charts. A good discipline, but don't come to rely on them, as they are by no means a crystal ball, because there are too many unknown factors. Undoubtedly the starting point though because, at the very least, it tells you what the market is doing right now, even if predicting the future, is another matter.

• Fundamentals of the company/coin - á la Warren Buffet's famous technique. He is a 'fundamental' investor, which basically means he knows the companies he invests in inside out. What's the TAM (total available market). Does it have a future? Does it have utility? Is it the only show in town? Are there real developer (dev) teams actually working on the coin or not? Many are dormant in that respect. Put the time in to find out.

• Stop and answer the fundamental question 'why is the market behaving this way today and what could it mean on the coming hours'. And it is hours, sometimes minutes, in Crypto. Be mindful (of what's going on) and have your own thoughts. There are a lot of narratives out there.

• Don't think you are invulnerable. You're not. Even if you are, it's not an excuse to be lazy.

• Write down your mistakes. Make a point of noting down what you got wrong and learn from it.

• Be aware of your upside and, more importantly, potential downside for every trade.

• Was the token issued in accordance with the law? Could it be subject to future action by the US or other authorities?

• News (real). Count on Twitter for the very latest. I follow over 1000 key players, and it's *the* place if you want up to the minute information. I keep mine Crypto-only. Obviously, there is a lot of noise to navigate, but I've bought Crypto and doubled my money in less than an hour, seeing news come out just minutes earlier. There are lots of other Crypto 'news' outlets, some better than others, but beware that many of the stories can be paid-for 'advertorial'.

• News (fake). Even fake news is worth paying attention to, as it too moves the market. All you really need to know is what direction it's going in and whether a particular falsehood will be believed and acted upon by the broader market or not.

• FUD – Fear Uncertainty and Doubt. This is usually sowed by the 'other side' – the banks, governments and naysayers. Stand firm, but beware that, like fake news, which it often is, FUD also affects markets.

• Don't just act, think - Just because people are saying it on their feed, or because somebody posted a miracle message on Facebook, doesn't mean it's true. Read the white paper yourself. Read anything you can find on the internet yourself. And don't forget to type into Google "is ABC-coin (or ABC-company) a scam". Those four words have served me well. Dig dig dig. Discover who are the founders are, then look them up individually. It's more common than you would think to have completely fake names and directors.

• If you're buying into a new ICO or another offering, as we've said, actually *read* the White Paper, but also even copy small chunks of text from it into Google. You'll soon see whether this is an original work or has just plagiarised from other White Papers. This is very common, and you know what to do if you find they've done this. Remember that you can do reverse image searches too; especially useful for photos of the apparent founders. It does happen, so tick it off the list, even if it's non-conclusive. Remember, it's real money you're laying down here.

• Don't allow yourself to be coerced. This comes back to 'don't believe the hype' again.

• Ethereum goes up and down quite sharply, depending on whether a big new ICO has been completed or not. This is because the recipient company for the investment will immediately start selling the pledged Ether to realise Fiat capital and kick off their start-up. Similarly, it will go up when investors are buying. So keep an eye on when the biggest fundraisers are.

• Tether or other 'stable coin' printing indicates that a large buy order might be going through soon. The trader is lining up the funds ready for a trade, just as they traditionally would when funding a Fiat broker account. However, with stable coins, this can be looked up on the stable coin's own blockchain explorer. In the case of Tether, you can see these issuances on the following ones – Blockchain, Omniexplorer, Etherscan and Tokenview.

• It's worth noting that stablecoins are rarely exactly worth their peg, which in the case of Tether is supposed to be $1. If there is nothing in the market pointing towards a big event, you might bet they will soon return to the peg. Small percentages of money can be made trading it before it does. Or play the arbitrage game and pick a different exchange with better prices for the same asset.

• Arbitrage, or the difference between prices on different exchanges. There are still significant price differences to be found, but this will settle as the market matures. Given the ease of moving cryptocurrencies from one wallet to another, why not move it around between different exchanges a bit as the price differs. Nothing wrong with that. If someone elsewhere wants to pay you a tiny bit more, or sell for a bit less, it would be rude not to accept. Be sure to factor in on-chain charges and be sure you know what fees you're paying too. It's not always apparent, but if you're careful who you use, and keep a dose of reality, you'll be fine.

• Changing government legislation worldwide. You can't shut Bitcoin down, now that the genie is out of the bottle, but sentiment can quickly change. Eyes open.

• Centralised government or bank-issued cryptocurrencies. These will still have the same flaws and security issues as Fiat money and any centralised offering. Undoubtedly this will affect the market as it matures, and more and more people adopt 'real' Crypto. But remember that the vast majority of the population believe what the government tells them and might be happy with this inferior version.

• Short selling or Contracts for Difference (CFD's). This tends to move market sentiment, just as Long selling does. Check out the open contracts being offered for yourself.

• Hold cash or crypto specifically to be available and at-the-ready when an opportunity arises.

• Hacks or security breaches. This always affects sentiment, but Bitcoin seems impervious. Most hacks are of individual customer accounts or exchange wallets that have not been adequately secured or have fallen foul to phishing attempts. Despite the many hacks of exchange funds so far, the price of Bitcoin is mostly unaffected, at least certainly in the long term. 12 years in, it has weathered storm after storm. In contrast, the naysayers have done their best to write it off, but failed.

• Time zones. Generally speaking, you can see the market movement in Crypto as each region awakes. Unlike the stock market (so far), crypto markets are open 24/7.

• Particular times of the month/year such as public holidays or even weekends deserve extra attention, of yourself too. Exuberance abounds, and happy (or sad) people make irrational decisions.

• Avoid boredom and especially making stupid decisions when bored. Walk away and come back later. You're not obliged to make a trade.

It's better not to trade at all than make impulsive wrong-headed decisions.

• Diversify. Don't put all your eggs in one basket and make sure that the tokens you own represent a diverse field of application in various fields.

• Flash crash limit orders. Because of algorithmic trading and the triggering of automatic orders, it's possible for the price of an asset to briefly crash in price, perhaps by up to 90%. This is a temporary technical anomaly. But if you already have a low priced limit order in place, it will execute and allow you to buy at the low price if the crash happens.

• Limit orders in general are a great way to bag a cheap deal if you're prepared to leave capital tied up waiting for the right price. It doesn't need to be in the flash-crash territory. Just leave the order sitting there. And you can alter your orders and offer prices as the market matures. When the price drops, even for seconds, your order should execute, and you've bought at a great price. Maybe you set the limit for 10-20% less than the market price of the asset. If you get lucky, you've just made 20%. If not, crucially, you have lost nothing, and it's a great way to have a seat at the table without necessarily staring at a screen all day.

• Performance of other investment markets. If the stock market tanks, then you are going to see a lot of people forced to make margin calls and possibly liquidate crypto assets to pay for it. Conversely, Bitcoin could become a safe haven for funds at difficult economic times, as it is wholly unburdened and unaffected with fiscal burden and the magic money printing machine.

• Don't believe the hype!!! How could we possibly forget that one!!! Unless you're intending to deliberately ride a fake wave one-footed, don't get caught up in a Twitter-storm of publicity. Always thoroughly check independent sources, or even just *other* sources. Avoid tacky candy-flossy marketing. Avoid car-salesman deals and impossible returns. If the thing is good enough, it'll stand on its own feet. This is your money we are talking about, not candy crush. Avoid. Avoid.

• Beware of the enormous risks and potential losses of leveraged trading. 5x, 10x, or even 100x your principal sum invested can just as quickly turn against you in seconds, and completely liquidate your position. In fact it has often ended in suicide. This is basically gambling, and you need to be even more sure of your facts if you don't want to lose your shirt. Additionally, anyone offering it without a full-scale banking license, not just a money transmitting one, is breaking the law. So you'll be walking on thin ice in more ways than one.

• Learn to control your emotions and never make decisions based on a knee-jerk reaction. Pause, think it through, keep calm and carry on. Warren Buffet said in 2003 "You wait for the fat pitch". Some of the old rules still apply - don't get emotional.

• FOMO or Fear Of Missing Out. Don't *necessarily* panic if there's a stampede. The market can overreact very fast, in either direction, especially now that people have all sorts of limit orders set to trigger. Be patient and don't fold at the first apparent bad hand. Believe in your hard work and research, and it shouldn't freak you out.

• Don't invest more than you can afford to lose. No matter how good you are, you don't have the power to predict every factor. Which of us could have predicted Covid-19? In all endeavours, there is always potential for a sidewinder to come out of nowhere. I don't care what the "You can do it if you believe you can" tribe says.

• HODL (Hold on for dear life). At the end of the day, consider just holding your prized digital assets for the long term. Or as crypto enthusiasts say - HODL. You can still put them to work for you, and it's easier to fund your trading with Crypto in any case. If you don't need to jump back in and out of Fiat, perhaps don't.

10. PRIVACY COINS

"All human beings have three lives: public, private, and secret."
Gabriel García Márquez, Columbian novelist.

There is a lot of talk about Bitcoin being the money of choice for criminals, drug gangs, people traffickers or worse. All of that is entirely possible. Of course Bitcoin is used for these things, just as US$ or Euros are used for these things. And roads and planes and just about anything we use legitimately. We don't ban roads because bank robbers can escape using them. Any new technology, particularly disruptive ones, will always find the bad players as well as the good. That's inevitable, unfortunately. However, credible estimations are that less than 2% of global transactions on the Bitcoin blockchain are for illicit purposes. That compares to around 15% in the world of cash that we know about.

The fact is, that far from being impossible to track, Bitcoin transactions are impossible to *hide*, as long as you know who the owner of the wallet is. Up to that point, and on the Blockchain, user wallets allow for pseudonymous ownership. That is to say, the public key associated with the wallet can be looked up if you know it. However, you don't necessarily also have the ability to connect that with a person or owner unless someone has told you it's their wallet. As a proof of work blockchain, you can simply look a wallet address up on the blockchain explorer. It will tell you all transactions in and out of that wallet, plus the other wallets' money that has come in and gone out too. So if I have 50 Bitcoin in my wallet, and ask you to pay into that wallet, you could find all that information out. It's not unreasonable that some people want a bit more privacy than that. After all, you wouldn't give a stranger your bank statement to peruse, would you? There's nothing dodgy about wanting to keep it private. It's normal.

Of course, anonymity is only possible if someone can't connect a wallet address to you, or to a network of other payments and wallets. Sophisticated tracking and analysis tools now exist to try to make those links. Still, you must be connected in some way to one of the wallet addresses in the chain. It's even possible to follow stolen Bitcoin as it passes between wallets, and companies such as 21 Analytics, Coinfirm and Chainalysis are experts at this. Many exchanges will now block a payment if it involves stolen funds. They're usually required to do so by the laws of their land, mind you. If privacy is vital, it's not a bad idea to use TOR anyway (the Onion Router), but at the end of the day, it was invented and released by the US Navy. Designed for undercover operatives, it would be impossible to hide their identity unless the general public worldwide were doing it too.

Consequently, a whole raft of privacy coins has developed, with Monero, Dash and Verge, all launched in 2014, leading the way. There are, in fact, over 70 of these coins, so here is a small but popular handful. You might not keep *all* your money in them, but you can move capital seamlessly between Bitcoin and any of this new breed of coins.

Monero XMR – Probably the safest, most popular and successful privacy coin. It uses multiple stealth addresses in the transaction, effectively blocking any trace. Also 'ring signatures', where the transaction can be signed by anyone in a group of people holding the key and not attributed to one person. No opt-in makes it safe from the outset.

Zcash ZEC uses a cryptographic technique known as Zero-knowledge proof. Both the transaction amount and the two wallet addresses are not revealed. Also, transactions are mixed together. However, it is not impossible to unravel transactions within Zcash, and this has been proved by firms such as Chainalysis. Users must opt-in for full privacy or risk disclosing their identity or IP address.

Dash DASH mixes multiple transactions (minimum of 3) and participants as one single transaction to make it impossible to track. Dash also suffers from the same issue as Zcash, and more sophisticated analysis tools are being developed all the time, discovering weaknesses. Also opt-in like Zcash, so vulnerable.

Verge XVG – Instead of relying on cryptographic techniques, Verge uses The Onion Router (TOR). It bounces the users' identities around the world, network to network, computer to computer, making it theoretically impossible to trace.

11. SAFE STORAGE OF ASSETS - WALLETS, PRIVATE SEEDS AND KEYS

"Not your keys, not your coins."
Andreas Antonopolous, leading Bitcoin advocate and educator

Between 2009 and 2013, British I.T. worker James Howells mined a total of 7,500 bitcoins on his laptop, while difficulty was still low enough to do this without enormous computing power. At the time, Bitcoins were still very cheap. When he eventually threw out his old laptop, he kept the old hard drive containing the coins, to one side. However, later that year, during a clear-out, he accidentally threw it away. The lost Bitcoins were worth an incredible $146 million at their peak. This wouldn't usually have been a problem, because all transactions are, as we know, stored forever in the Blockchain and thus recoverable with the private key. However, this went directly to a landfill in Wales, with the hard drive, so any kind of recovery was impossible. And, because 50,000 tons of waste is added to the site every year, the likelihood of it ever being recovered is virtually nil. So they've now stopped him digging (well, wouldn't *you* search). We are always losing passwords in everyday life but lose your private keys, and they're gone forever - along with all your money. No 'password reset' here.

"So, how do I keep my cryptocurrency safe?" you might reasonably ask. Well, as secure and stable as the code is, you still rely upon the safety of your private key. It's the single, most critical, thing to keep safe. This, however, is a 64-character string that would test the memory of a magician, even if you did feel safe to commit it to memory alone. But if you lose it, you lose the money forever. Well, you have very few options, depending on where you are going to keep your coins. Here's an example of a private key:

E9873D79C6D87DC0FB6A5778633389F4453213303DA61F20BD67F-
C233AA33262

Not especially snappy or easy to remember, I think you'll agree. Accordingly, digital wallet providers offer the alternative of remembering a 'seed phrase'. This is 12 or 24 ordinary English language words in sequence. Logging into your wallet is then just a case of remembering your seed phrase, typing in a selection of these words on request. Even so, it's not very easy to remember, and you probably end up writing it down on a piece of paper anyway.

Tyler and Cameron Winklevoss describe, in Ben Mezrich's fantastic book 'Bitcoin Billionaires', how they secured the paper keys to hundreds of millions of dollars' worth of Bitcoin. The book is a wonderful narrative of the whole story and I highly recommend a read. The twin brothers are famous for being co-creators of Facebook, and subsequently suing Mark Zuckerberg (successfully) for coming up with the idea. Since then, they've been evangelists for Bitcoin and front runners in helping widespread adoption increase, and run the compliant Gemini exchange out of New York. The two picked bank vaults in four different banking groups spread out geographically around the United States. The keys are written on paper, cut in half, duplicated four times, and spread across the vaults. This way, if somebody did manage to get hold of one of the pieces, or one of the banking groups went under, was robbed, or was swallowed by an earthquake, their keys would still be completely safe. They even went to the extraordinary step of smashing up the equipment used to store or print the keys - computers and even printers.

This isn't really a very easy method, to say the least, from something on the cutting edge of digital technology! What irony. However, in reality, it's currently the only way if you want to be sure. At the time, the Winklevoss twins had bought 120,000 Bitcoins at around the $10 mark, and they were worth more than 2 billion dollars. You'd want to be damn sure it was safe.

New protocols that make life simpler will almost certainly be developed, as in the early development of the web and the switch from long IP addresses to URL's.

Currently, you have a few options of where to put your coins.

• Phone wallet. Store on a software wallet on your phone - there are many wallets out there, most of them open-source, so you know the code is public and verifiably safe. But do you really want to keep all your wealth on a connected device? It's a great way of carrying - say - $1000 worth to pay or transfer easily, but you wouldn't draw out all your life savings in cash and carry it with you.

• Desktop computer wallet. Store on a software wallet on your computer - Similarly this is not a particularly secure way either, at least if your computer is connected to the internet. As with a phone wallet, it works well and makes life easy, however, simply isn't secure enough to risk leaving all your wealth on there.

• Exchange. Store on an exchange online - many people just leave the Cryptocurrency on an exchange, perhaps even the same one you bought the coins. Now you're taking a significant risk, maybe the worst kind of risk, and it's a very lazy way to do it. Sure, it allows for instant funds to cover buy orders that might be triggered, for example, but it's not safe. There have already been multiple hacks into exchanges that are well documented.

• Air-gapped computer wallet. Store on a software wallet on an air-gapped computer - This is somewhat better all-round, though not easily-adopted by the mainstream. Take a laptop and strip out the wi-fi card. You effectively have an air-gapped device that can't be accessed from anywhere other than being physically with the machine.

• Hardware Cold Wallet. The #1 most secure method. Several companies are selling cold storage devices which look similar to a memory stick but contain a processing SE chip (Secure Element). It has its own operating system and a small amount of memory to hold the wallet software for each coin and the public keys. They're all inexpensive, usually well under $100. I would recommend that you don't buy from a third party, even Amazon, as there is a slim possibility of back doors or malware being installed. Direct from the manufacturer is the best practice. There is no connection via wi-fi, no Bluetooth, and barely enough memory to leave room for malware on the device anyway. You do need to plug it in via USB at the moment of any transfer, but this is limited and encrypted, and verification of transfer takes place on the cold device itself. A cold wallet in any form (memory stick, hard drive, server) is currently the safest way to store and move cryptocurrencies. Commercial examples are Ledger, Keep key and market leader Trezor. It does still represent a risk, but that risk is significantly mitigated. As we said at the beginning of this chapter - Not your keys, not your coins.

If you can't go to the lengths that the Winklevoss brothers went to, it's relatively easy to find inventive places you can safely keep your paper 'written-down' key. For example, go to your bookshelf, pick a couple of favourite books, split the key in two, remember the page numbers, and write down your key in two places in the book. Or even in two separate books in different rooms. It's better than nothing, and even if someone knew you held coin, it would take a very long time to find. Assuming you have a fair few books.

Whatever you do, that private key is God. Be disciplined and lock it down, even if that's sometimes inconvenient. It's your money we are talking about, so it's better to sacrifice a bit of easiness for a lot of safety.

12. WHO'S AFRAID OF THE BIG, BAD WOLF?

"Came the day when fate did frown
And a wolf blew into town
With a gruff huff puff, he puffed just enough
And the hay house fell right down."
Frank Churchill and Ann Ronell

I'll put you out of your misery, this chapter is about the law. I'm reasonably confident no-one has ever quoted 'the Three Little Pigs' in a legal context before! But take it as a metaphor for the crumbling old money system, or the arrival of Crypto and Blockchain. Or perhaps even the fact that law enforcement has been slow to catch on but is now on steroids. All three are true. I'm not an advocate of the legal system, nor am I a legal advocate. But, while that might be true, laws are there. They just are. And their masters are starting to huff and puff too. Listening to many in crypto-land, you would think they were living in their own made-up Utopia. A Utopia it can be, and indeed is well on the way to being, but we aren't quite there yet.

Equally, it doesn't make me a criminal using Bitcoin or any other cryptocurrency. Sensible governments know that a ban would be futile anyway, as it's impossible to stop. But existing financial laws cross over. There's a fight over whether they even apply to the world of Crypto. Especially where a country can't even decide if it's money or a commodity, subject to sales tax or anything else. But there are plenty of *legal* ways to go forward, assuming you want to go that way. Why make life difficult for yourself. Like I say, Cryptocurrency in itself is legal in most places in the world. Thankfully some countries haven't knee-jerked, and laws are evolving sensibly in co-operation with the industry. The world into which Bitcoin has been deployed is immense, as befits a real contender to be *the* world reserve currency. If that happened, consider the wealth that would pour in, and the ensuing value of every Bitcoin. According to Google, the total wealth of the *world* is $360.6 trillion. However, I have no idea how that can possibly be a credible figure. Okay, I admit, I am getting ahead of myself. Besides, Bitcoin is about more than tawdry 'market value'. Though, to be clear, there's no shame in tawdry market value, I can't lie. It's a pleasant thought anyway. Bitcoin without borders, though, is genius. Because of that impartiality, Bitcoin literally acting as the book-keeper for the entire world's wealth is not entirely inconceivable, either. It's also 'of its time', especially as the west slams the door in the face of global trade and co-operation. Our fundamental rights to privacy and control have somehow been milked away. Thankfully, we just have to rely on each other as individuals en-masse. That's not actually too tough these days, and anyway Bitcoin helps us with this also.

When the US introduced the Patriot Act in 2001, after 9/11, privacy disappeared in a puff of smoke, and our money became a public matter almost immediately. Strict anti-money-laundering (AML) and counter-terrorist financing (CTF) rules came into force over the next decade. They've only been strengthened over time, as they've been written into law worldwide. This is called KYC or Know Your Customer. All Fintech companies are subject to strict rules if they are holding public customer funds or dealing with members of the public. This does not apply to corporate entities, however, as the theory goes that they should know better than mere mortals like you and me. The classic argument goes "Well if you have nothing to hide, what's the harm". Indeed, that is true, and I don't want to enable criminals either, but what, then, is next? Will we be told and monitored how and when we spend our hard-earned money? That's entirely possible if central governments create their own twisted version of Crypto. I'll call that digital-Fiat, the digiDollar, digiPound, digiPeso, etc., because that's all it will be, still with all the inflationary, spending and borrowing issues of the past. Not to mention the same people tightly controlling it. *Hmm, I don't think I want your money any more. I'll take this other, much better, kind of money. Thanks though.*

Against this backdrop, for over a decade, Crypto companies have been able to do whatever they wanted. The authorities either didn't understand it, or didn't care, because they simply didn't have the vision to see the potential. It took a long time (perhaps 6 years) for lawmakers to get their head around the subject. That's nearly always the way with new tech. If you needed proof of that, remember that we are still arguing about whether Facebook and Google have to take any responsibility for their actions. So, to this day, most national governments have only come up with a framework of advisory suggestions. Some, led by Switzerland's Zug Canton or Crypto Valley, or Malta and Estonia, already have friendly laws. But the majority of the world is still way behind. Governments, however, do what they want, and many high-profile players are being prosecuted already. Much of this prosecution centres around the 'illegal' sale of digital tokens, as we mentioned in chapter 8, because of strict securities laws. It just took the SEC a while to catch on and catch up, but now they are in full caught-ON mode. And, of course, because of international treaties, in practice, the US really can do what it wants where its own citizens are involved. It will rigidly enforce its own rules and ride into any overseas territory it pleases.

In actual fact, oversight is a good thing for most people. However, promoting the 'regulated' route is not a popular path in the Crypto space, especially with libertarian views suggesting that anything goes. But in reality, what you actually *need* is oversight. I really do want to know that someone is watching what a company does with my money. Even if it has to be the government that's watching for now. Many have lost their money precisely because there was no oversight for years. Some unregulated exchanges and crypto intermediates made fortunes betting with other people's money. Just like the greedy bankers before them. Operating on tiny fractional reserves, they're only found out when already checkmated. No thanks.

Crypto was meant to usher in an era of control over our own funds, and you'll be glad to discover that it will still do that in the long run. Mainly by liberating us from the burden of central bank money, that always goes to zero in the end. Thanks to Bitcoin, I can still send funds anywhere in the world directly anyway. I don't even need to get involved with a third-party company, let's never forget that. What a concept. Thank you, Satoshi.

Nowadays, you'd have to shut down the internet and any other global networking to shut down Bitcoin. Despite a strong belief in personal freedoms, I don't ever want to be in the business of enabling terrorists, criminals and tax dodgers, or any organisation that encourages that, do you? But I do believe that the vast majority of society does good things with the freedoms they are given, and this applies here. But does that mean that our money should be anybody else's business but our own? I still don't think so, and at least now we have that option.

As miraculous as Bitcoin is, and deserving of the praise lavished upon it, I've tried to express the importance of sometimes looking on the other side of that wave of euphoria. Of being aware of potential bad players. If they won't allow themselves to be audited and are shrouded in mystery, potentially that's not a good thing, right? If you let your guard down, you're just asking for trouble. So if you get into Crypto as a business or investment, and you're not transacting directly on the Blockchain, let's say trading, I strongly suggest you use a company with oversight and regulation. Or at least one that's audited by a credible third party. Even if it's their local government. Yeah, I know that statement isn't going to go down well in some circles, but, hey, it's your money, and it's your choice. Feel free to...chow down on a complete unknown... because it's underground... exciting... or the latest buzz.

Back in the day you could get on a commercial flight to Geneva with a suitcase of money, pick a bank, any bank, and give them a number. But now Switzerland has complied with much international law and cleaned up its act. It's also trying to maintain privacy and autonomy, and does not roll over easily to outside 'authorities'. Almost certainly that's a good thing. The country has since been the leader in creating a sensible legislative Blockchain framework to work from, and is in direct and constant consultation with the Crypto industry itself. Again, I apologise if the words 'sensible legislation' grate on you. I do understand. But it's critical for mainstream adoption. Note that I did, at least, include the word 'sensible'.

Whatever your views, the reality is that there are strict rules now, and you can either decide to break them or flow with them and navigate a sensible way through. The alternative is to give your money to an unregulated company and risk losing it all. They might take it from you, or a government might take it from them. Either way, that's not a good scenario, and it's one that has already been played out more than once in both instances. Also, just because cryptocurrencies are secure and immutable, they can still just be handed over if the government metaphorically puts a gun to your head. Or, worse, because somebody else literally puts a gun to your head. Authorities have recently tracked down a 'missing billion' from the dark-market Silk Road. This was legally forfeited by a private key holder 7 years after its founder, Ross Ulbright, at age 31, went to jail for.. forever. Legally forfeited. That means: "You're nicked. Give us your private keys please, or we'll put you in the worst jail we can find, until the second coming". Ross was an extremely bright star, and hero of decentralisation to many, but he was breaking the law, it has to be said. It's a shame that he didn't put that great mind and vision towards something else in the space, but that's fate. His incredibly unjust *five* prison sentences are one more sad example of what happens if you take on the government and lose. For those not already acquainted, Ross is serving 20 years, 15 years, 5 years, and two life sentences, back-to-back. Ross fought the law and... The law won.

Obviously the unregulated route is your only option at the moment, if you don't want your ID checking and recording, at least. But let's get some perspective. Money isn't just another product, like buying stuff on Amazon. Is it really worth risking your funds for this small compromise? The crypto world is awash with people complaining about it. Still, as we've seen, they complain harder when their funds are gone forever, or their 'hero' is dragged to jail from half-way around the world. Happily, there are several blockchains, including ADA Cardano, that are working on embedded verification systems. Blockchain is the *perfect* technology for this, and significant steps will definitely be made in this area soon. It's the only way to go. Remember, using a distributed ledger on a blockchain we don't need a trusted third party to verify what we are saying is true. That means your data is safe and can't be sold on, even by the creator of the Blockchain. That would be a mild relief, wouldn't it? It's fit for, and used only for, purpose. Identify me, sure, then move on and don't make me pull my pants down.

How can the law look in the future? At the moment, that's my back yard. I'm a Brit and Swiss resident of Zug, where the best example is currently being set. I've been here for four years, recently building a cryptocurrency trading platform, where trades will legally take place 'on Swiss soil' on servers there. Anyway, the point is, that we want it to be legit, and that legal clarity is here already. Zug is a pleasant town about 30 minutes south of Zurich in the north of the country and has picked up the nickname 'Crypto Valley'. Sitting on a lake and surrounded by mountains, it has become the leading centre for Blockchain and Cryptocurrency firms in the world. It is here that the Ethereum Foundation is based, along with over 400 blockchain companies. And it is here that the majority of early ICO's were carried out and new laws explored. It's a good blueprint for other countries or regions to follow, and many are doing so.

Back in 2013, the cantonal (county) government saw the potential of Bitcoin and Blockchain before any other country, quickly making Bitcoin legal tender with no fuss. You can pay your taxes in Bitcoin if you like. Buy a rail ticket right on the platform too. I've even donated Crypto to a busking musician who had QR codes to his Bitcoin and Ethereum wallets on a laminated sheet. Yes, Bitcoin has even disrupted the traditional 'hat' money-collecting-device! Crypto at its purest, without intermediaries. I doubt that this man on Bahnhofstrasse in Zurich was likely to starve that night, but in those places where he might, say in Africa, Crypto has massive potential for inclusion in the financial landscape. Switzerland, for one, did not recognise Bitcoin as a threat to the regular money supply, since it represented only a tiny fraction of total supply (and still does for now). That said, the country does not borrow heavily against its currency, which is arguably the most stable in the world. If I had to pick a Fiat currency, the CHF would be it, certainly not the dollar and definitely not the Euro. But I don't have to pick one, and neither do you.

The example has been taken much further to present a robust, transparent, working environment for the new technology to have the space to grow. Coming to a town near you soon? Let's hope so. Many other countries are still deciding what to do about it, including the UK, while Zug sits at the forefront of building a workable legal framework. Yet, like any other country, there are strict rules, set out by the Swiss Anti Money Laundering and Terrorist Financing Act (AMLA), but they're always going to be there. Deal with it. The Swiss way of doing things is surprisingly democratic and consultative. In fact, with only 100,000 signatures, you can call a national and legally-binding referendum on anything you like. 'Total silence on a Wednesday' if you can drum up the interest. Actually, that wouldn't surprise me. You can't recycle, hang out washing, wash your car or mow your lawn on a Sunday as it is. Motorsport is banned, and apparently you can't ski down a mountain while reciting poetry, though I don't know why you would. The Swiss successfully complete about eight popular referendums every year. 400 in the last 50 years. I'm saying nothing about referendums, I'm British. We don't know how to do it. Crucially, these local laws almost always take precedence over national ones (Federal government). So consequently each canton chooses its own future and set its laws to suit a particular chosen industry. It actually goes to the root of Switzerland's tribal beginnings, where small mountain peoples, cut off from the rest of Europe, had to look out for themselves. The Swiss Federation, as a country, didn't exist until 1848, when those 'tribes', now cantons, came together. And now, in the 21st century, the canton of Zug has chosen to embrace Crypto and Blockchain. That's why, so far, it's one of the best places in the world for companies in the space. It's what we all want and need everywhere, going forward.

The main point to take away is this; just because a company or individual is excruciatingly, achingly cool and making up its own rules as it goes along, it doesn't mean they will be around tomorrow. Or, for that matter, that their ideas are sound, even if 'everybody' is saying they are. And that means they or the authorities can, and often do, take your money with them. There are several high profile and ongoing cases brought by the Securities and Exchange Commission (SEC) in the US against companies and individuals in the space. And with good reason. Many firms, exchanges particularly, blatantly flout the rules and their customers are none the wiser, until they get shut down of course. Some engage in 'front-running' and 'wash-trading', while others provide fake liquidity to make it look like the coin is in demand. That's basically straight-up stealing from their customers. Let's not call it anything else. Binance even offers this as a paid service for its customers and charges up to $6 million just to list a shitcoin. Legal shutdowns have already happened in several high-profile cases, and many ordinary people have lost money as a result. Even Switzerland is currently investigating over 60 companies.

Russian exchange BTC-e is one such firm that felt the full force of the US authorities. It didn't ask where the customers got their money, nor ask anything about them. This seems great at first, even when you're not a criminal. Why should I give you my details anyway, let you check my passport, and potentially present these details to the authorities? What a load of hassle. But that's not the point. The point is that you can be fleeced if there is no authority oversight. There is nothing to stop fake volumes pumping the price and your money being used to invest in risky trades that profit the exchange and not you. Who's looking after all?! For years, people traded freely on BTC-e, and many left their coins on the exchange too (including a close friend who should have known better). *Never leave more than you need to trade with on an exchange long term.* But in 2017, founder Alexander Vinnik was arrested while on vacation in Greece, for fraud, having been accused on 21 counts of laundering almost two billion dollars. He is also charged with handling funds stolen from the hack of the first Crypto exchange ever - Mt Gox in Japan (which also famously collapsed). Despite being an exchange supposedly based in Eastern Europe, the BTC-e site and the crypto-assets were stored in the cloud. US Authorities were able to just walk into a data centre in California and physically pull the servers. Simple.

Authorities took nearly 40% of all funds, and every single customer lost money.

One of the issues is that most countries do not have set rules about whether cryptocurrencies are even legal tender. Is it a security, is it a commodity, is it subject to sales tax, is it money or not? They just can't decide. So many businesses tend to go to a country where there are no rules. Most western countries have issued strong warnings, but not written proper legislation into law yet, but a tidal wave is coming. You just need to be on the right side of it. This only serves to show how useful decentralisation and Bitcoin is, though. Notably, China banned all crypto activities, except mining, before testing its own state-controlled Fiat and centralised Cryptocurrency. Russia did the same. The island of Malta, though, has been progressive, writing articles into law that make it a favoured destination to trade. However, in 2019, the Prime Minister, Joseph Muscat, had to step down to avoid allegations that he had participated in the murder of a journalist there. I don't know about you, but it doesn't exactly inspire confidence.

The fact is that there are many companies operating today where you know nothing about the beneficial owners. Admittedly that's something Switzerland and the UK are good at. But at best they're based in a dodgy country or tax haven. Not that there's anything intrinsically wrong with that. Nobody can know whether customer deposits are still there if the operation is running on fractional reserves. This is great for them, but it puts your money at risk, and they could be shut down or subpoenaed at any time. This brings us, shorty, to the case of Bitfinex, who 'lost' nearly a billion dollars of customer funds because their payment processor was a mafia controlled company in Panama (Crypto Capital). It's all true. Bitfinex was the biggest exchange in the world at the time, and, incredibly, still are a significant player. Going down this kind of dark alleyway does not make sense, no matter how much money you're making.

If it was my money I would actually like to know if there is a trusted authority, government or otherwise, that is overseeing it. I can know that my money is actually still there, for one thing, and they can't use it to bet with - only to lose badly.

So our final example illustrates this point very well; looking at the affairs of well-known exchange Bitfinex, and it's 'stable coin' US Dollar Tether (USDT). The latter is supposed to be backed one to one with real dollars in a separate bank account, so the value always remains the same. A solid idea, as stable coins have the potential to allow for faster trades and more seamless transacting. However, the firm has always refused legitimate audits to prove this. Still, incredibly, people use the Cryptocurrency daily across multiple exchanges. In 2018, as regulators closed in, legitimate banking sources, one by one, were closed to them. Bitfinex started using a mafia-controlled company in Panama called Crypto Capital. And, shock-surprise, a massive $850 million went 'missing'. Whether this was from speculation with other people's money or simply theft, is still to be revealed in the courts. Bitfinex asserts that it was taken by the mafia and/or Panamanian government. Either way, in a desperate attempt to plug the hole, Bitfinex stole the funds from its USDT account and is now subject to ongoing legal action by authorities in the US. Even so, people *still* use the exchange and the 'Tether' currency, even when it seems only a matter of time before the whole thing collapses. In the electronic age, the market for it could collapse in minutes, and is unlikely to give you any way out, nor a market to dump it on. Nobody will be buying. As for Bitfinex and USDT refunding you from its '1:1 treasury'? Dream on. Make sure you're amongst the first in the queue, because the money doesn't exist. If it did, we would all have seen proof.

Some ICO's haven't escaped the authorities' wrath either. Many have been classified as Securities offerings within the letter of the law. Consequently, it needs to be carried out legitimately, with proper KYC (Know your Customer), proper prospectuses and authorisation. Otherwise, the US is forcing companies to refund US customers their investments. Do they really know if the money is still there? If that happens and you've bought the token with the expectation of a price increase, it will likely kill the investment.

We are at a turning point where, thankfully, the market is maturing, and the bad players are being rooted out. New (and old) rules are starting to be followed. This is, without a doubt, the best thing that can happen to Crypto and Blockchain. It's the only way forward if it is to have any hope of gaining mass appeal. More and more people want to adopt Crypto in a sensible, safe environment. Bitcoin and Crypto is not going anywhere any time soon. With only 21 million Bitcoin to go around, perhaps it's time to get yours now, if you haven't already.

13. DECENTRALISED FINANCE (DEFI) AND THE FUTURE

"I know not what weapons World War III will be fought, but World War IV will be fought with sticks and stones."
Albert Einstein, famous clever guy.

I realise that quote is barely relevant, but I like it, and perhaps the democratisation of money will help to prevent this vision from becoming inevitable. We are certainly at a tipping point where technology is catching up with Sci-Fi, and we do need to use it wisely if we are not to be trampled by it. One thing's for sure: the creator(s) of Bitcoin weren't warmongers. And most people in this space, those who are actually creating something, care deeply about being on the right side of history.

I promised you a book without the bullshit, so if I come down hard on some things, it's because it has to be said. Someone has to be balanced. Crypto-world, like most others, is not perfect. Despite the sometimes crude candy-flossy marketing, the pitfalls are mostly fairly obvious. Often precisely *because* of the candy-flossy marketing. Bitcoin itself continues to provide a safe store of value, possibly even a future world-reserve currency. Nobody can stop it. Or any other coin based on a distributed ledger. It's out there, and that's that.

John McAfee, namesake and ex-patron of the Anti-virus software, is not averse to a bit of hype. He has been criticised for pushing his favourite crypto tokens to his ever-enthusiastic fans. Oh, and for refusing to pay US taxes. But he is nevertheless a colourful and intelligent voice for the industry. In 2017 he famously stated that if Bitcoin hadn't reached a value of half a million dollars by 2020 "I'll eat my dick on national television". He then doubled down on his bet and upped it to a million dollars. It didn't, and neither did he. But many believe there is no reason why this couldn't play out eventually, myself included. Not the dick eating, obviously. I don't mean in fifty years either. Maybe in five or ten though. Thank you for the satire and confidence, John. Glad you didn't go through with it though.

The fastest-growing movement in Blockchain has, without doubt, been decentralised finance - or DeFi. Essentially, this is what we've been discussing in this book. The reason for that is simple – Blockchain and decentralisation is the perfect solution for the future of money. Money for 'us' anyway, money that benefits real people. Many legacy financial instruments are being replaced by a blockchain equivalent, and the decentralised, trustless nature of Blockchain is changing the landscape forever. Soon we will be saying goodnight to some of the more cumbersome corporations of the past. DeFi dares to dream that dream.

DeFi now offers operations like lending and borrowing, staking, dividend or interest-bearing coins, payment systems, derivatives, stablecoins, blockchain-bonds and the eventual tokenisation of *all* assets on stock exchanges too. Everything and more. If it's been done in regular finance, it's being done in DiFi. Just holding some coins will give the bearer interest sometimes exceeding 10%. Whether this is a verifiable return or just a near-Ponzi reward for buying yet another shitcoin, is a very fine line. In fact, strictly speaking, any asset giving interest or dividends is subject to strict financial regulation. It's very likely to ultimately be classified as a security, and possibly even shut down if it doesn't comply. You have to ask yourself, though, in a world of negative interest rates and low liquidity, exactly *how* does it legitimately provide that kind of return on investment.

So, as always, from an investor's point of view, you must investigate the company thoroughly, and decide whether its activities are subject to laws and regulations in *your* country. Even if the company is based somewhere else. I'm no stuffed-shirt, but, like it or not, most are. Many early ICO projects are being taken out by the SEC in America, and other financial authorities. It's only a resource issue stopping them going after many more. The Defi world will come under the same scrutiny, despite often having altruistic reasons for circumventing the legal framework. I don't like this heavy hand any more than you do, as it can stifle innovation, but you must be on the right side of it. In any case, nobody could argue whether Crypto has attracted a lot of bad players, or that many have lost money directly because of the lack of oversight. The early days of Crypto felt very much like a wild west, and I won't deny, felt very exciting. Companies thought themselves invincible. They thought they could do whatever they wanted, but the sad fact is that they can't.

Decentralised is not always decentralised either, just because it's today's buzzword or that someone says it is. If the data is not stored and reconciled on a distributed decentralised ledger, with incentivised miners, then it's basically still a legacy financial instrument. This is when they can and do come unstuck. Many many projects are controlled by a corporate entity and board of directors and not by a community or DAO (Decentralised Organisation). Even some DAO's are essentially little more than an extended board of directors. This is not decentralised. And if it isn't open-source, out there for all to use and inspect, and distributed across servers worldwide, then it isn't decentralised either. In fact, after an excellent start to 2020, with some DeFi tokens gaining value by 10 or 20 times their value (10x or 20x). September saw them lose up to 60% of their value just as Bitcoin started to gain traction again. The seasoned Crypto expert will recognise this pattern, as it is very often the case. Tokens increase dramatically in value, then slump back by about 60% of that high regularly, as people take profits and sell into the market. Even Bitcoin has followed that pattern in the early years. But it's always up overall, and has been much more stable lately.

Even so-called Decentralised Exchanges are not strictly so. Suppose the company at the heart of it takes custody of any asset for even a millisecond. In that case, they are subject to financial regulations and anti-money-laundering checks. It's my belief that many of these companies will be prosecuted in the coming months. People talk of decentralised exchange, or Atomic Swaps, but this is still not possible cross-chain (from one Blockchain to a different one). One solution would be a universal protocol change to every single Blockchain to enable them to communicate. That's not happened yet. Most DEX (digital exchange) takes place between the various assets on the Ethereum blockchain, but not outside it, or on an alternative smart contracting platform. Sometimes other assets like Bitcoin are represented by an Ethereum token, for the purposes of exchange. This is called 'wrapping'. However, somewhere somebody usually still has to convert that centrally into Bitcoin itself or into FIAT money. That's when it becomes subject to the law. That's when your money is hanging in the wind if it's with a company operating on sketchy ground.

Nevertheless, Decentralised Exchange has increased dramatically since 2019. 2020 saw DEX volumes multiply by more than ten times year-on-year to over $25 billion a month. Impressive, but it still has a long way to catch the volumes and liquidity (available buyers and sellers) of centralised exchanges like Coinbase and Kraken. Bitcoin alone 'centrally' trades over twice that amount - per day. For now, DEX seems to have largely escaped the eye of regulators around the world but watch this space as that market share increases and the tech develops. I believe its time will come though, even if the key blockchains don't collectively agree upon a future protocol in their code to allow for it. When it realises its promise, DEX really could sidestep governments and fulfil its original de-central-ised promise.

While there are now many new coins and projects out there, Bitcoin has weathered countless storms and always come out on top. After all, it is over 12 years old. Though it undoubtedly does go down in value as well as up, overall it has increased far more than any other asset in the world - every single year. In fact, throughout the whole of 2020, Bitcoin started to look like a remarkably stable asset, without the wild swings that categorised its early years. And don't forget that its scarcity, balanced with real and growing demand, gives it long-term value. That is why I say that it will be here for a long time to come.

Following the economic collapse surrounding the coronavirus crisis, more and more corporate entities, national banks and fund managers have started the hedge their bets with exposure to Bitcoin. Famously, payment provider Square, owned by Jack Dorsey, founder of Twitter, put $50 million with Bitcoin in October 2020. Nasdaq listed Microstrategy has all of its $425m reserves in Bitcoin now too, after already investing $250m back in August 2020. There is widespread confidence in Bitcoin's value going forward. Many other firms and individuals have done the same. In fact, there are now well over 1600 Bitcoin wallets with over a million dollars-worth in them.

Whether or not Bitcoin becomes the fungible day-to-day payment system that Satoshi Nakamoto wanted, remains to be seen. But it is undoubtedly a safe store of assets, like digital gold, except better. Now it is all but legitimised by many organisations and the public at large. 'Layer-2' technologies are being built in a frenzy of creativity, further fuelling the fire. Even Banks, central and otherwise, and governments are trying to get in on the act. Soon they too will introduce their own versions of Bitcoin – except all with the same faults and issues of their regular Fiat counterparts. Crypto stalwart, Simon Dixon, is author of the book Bank to the Future, an ex banker and crypto fundraiser. His book accurately predicted this future back in 2012 and he has more to say on the subject. If I could follow just one person, he would be it. For at least a year now, he has been predicting that the banks will take the opportunity of electronic currency to get themselves out of the massive hole they've dug for themselves. Since all banks operate legally on fractional reserves of just 8% or so of customer money, and many have started operating on zero reserves (also legal now), they are basically bankrupt. Mr Dixon thinks that when the fit hits the shan, they, or perhaps the central bank, will issue new digital currency and hand it out to their customers in lieu of the money they owe us all. Of course, this is creating money out of thin air again, something which they have been doing for the last century. Also, imagine a world where the state controls your money electronically. What if you're given a benefit to spend on travel, let's say, will you be required to actually spend that money the way they want? Will our identities and ability to conduct transactions be removed if we don't pay our taxes on time? Personally I don't like the sound of it.

Banks and legacy institutions aside, there is now deep liquidity in key crypto markets, and so many players involved, that Bitcoin is now highly unlikely to lose value and traction. There are always buyers and sellers, and there will always be free-market forces and free thinkers. Bitcoin and Blockchain can be whatever we want to make it. Whatever we want to build on top of it. It's an inclusive world that nearly anyone can get involved in. It breaks down the barriers of the establishment and offers us all autonomous control over our own money and many other aspects of life. In short, it is real freedom and democracy. Us, not them. How you use this opportunity is up to you.

14. FULL GLOSSARY OF TERMS

2FA - 2 Factor Authentication. Extra security sign-in measures to avoid your exchange account being hacked (in this case). Recommended at every single opportunity, however inconvenient. Receive verification by SMS or use an app like Google's Authy (preferable) to verify that it's really you. If you use SMS, you need to lock down your sim with your mobile provider in a similar way, so nobody can just clone it.

51% attack - If mining groups control 51% of all the computing hash power, a blockchain can be attacked and unravelled. This is extremely hard to achieve with a large blockchain like Bitcoin, but smaller chains have occasionally been attacked in this way.

Altcoin - A cryptocurrency that isn't Bitcoin. Bitcoin was first, but there are now thousands of derivative coins with different ideas and mandates.

AML - Anti Money Laundering. Worldwide laws that verify identity, origin, and movement of funds.

ASIC - Application Specific Integrated Circuit. Custom chips used in mining hardware and cold storage wallets.

ATH – All time high. The highest price a coin has reached in its lifetime.

Bagholder/ Bags – Person holding a large amount of tokens (bag of tokens) living in the hope that the price will go up in the longer term. Not necessarily used in a positive context, as many will be stuck with a dormant token that will never recover, 'holding their bags'.

Bitcoin Jesus - Name given to Bitcoin enthusiast Roger Ver. Ver contributed a lot to promote Bitcoin early adoption and has now firmly planted his belief in Bitcoin Cash (BCH), the hard fork created in Aug 2007.

Block - In the case of Bitcoin, a block contains approximately 10 minutes' worth of transactions. These are 'hashed' together in a block and added to the Blockchain.

Blockchain - All the transactions ever produced in a 'Proof-Of-Work' blockchain like Bitcoin's. Each block is added to the chain by hashing together. Impossible to alter or unravel without all the nodes in the system taking part.

CBDC - Central Bank Digital Currency. As the name suggests, a centralised government cryptocurrency. The only problem is that a CBDC has the same issues as a FIAT currency, as money supply and value is decided by those in charge. So it's just a digital FIAT. China was the first country to test their Digital yuan, and major western governments will be next.

CFD - Contract for Difference. Allows investors to participate in price movement without owning the Cryptocurrency (or stock, or foreign currency). Owners of the contracts can decide to go long or short the asset, meaning they are betting on whether it will go up or down in value over time. A counterparty to the contract will underwrite that risk, and smart contracting is a particularly secure way of doing this in the crypto world.

Cold or hardware wallet - Hardware device, usually about the size of a memory stick, that can be air-gapped from the internet (not connected). The wallet is only connected momentarily at the point of transferring coins. Very secure, but it's vital to realise that it's more important to keep your private key or phrase safe at all times. Even if you lose or break the device, you can then retrieve your coins directly from the Blockchain or restore them to a replacement wallet of any kind.

Cryptocurrency - A form of money secured electronically by cryptography.

Cryptography - Literally meaning 'hidden writing', cryptographic techniques protect information and communications so that only the intended person can read them. Has been around since long before the days of computing.

CTF - Counter-Terrorist Financing. Hand in hand with AML, it uses techniques and monitoring to prevent money from being used for terrorist organisations.

DAO - Decentralised Autonomous Organisation. Decisions are made democratically, with the participation of a community of users, rather than a single company or person.

Dapps - Decentralised apps that are running on a blockchain like Ethereum or others. The code is open source and can be copied and replicated. Decisions are reached by consensus and not a centralised authority.

Decentralisation - An organisation or protocol requiring no trusted central authority, which is used in some, but by no means all, cryptocurrency or software applications.

DeFi – Decentralised Finance is the new movement dedicated to replacing legacy financial systems with decentralised and transparent protocols. If they are genuinely decentralised, they run semi democratically, without the need for any intermediary.

Desktop wallet - a software wallet hosted on your PC, but still connected to the internet unless the wi-fi card is removed, thus making it a cold storage device.

Distributed ledger - A ledger record of transactions (financial in the case of Bitcoin) that is distributed amongst thousands of computers, each holding an identical copy. As such, it is impossible to fake records or hack the system without all 'nodes' participating. Far more secure than keeping files on a central or single server. Bitcoin has nearly 100,000 nodes already, and anyone can operate one.

DLT – Distributed Ledger Technology.

Double Spend - A problem that pre-dates, and was solved by, Bitcoin, where a person can spend the same electronic coin twice. This is now not possible unless the counterparty to a transaction accepts an unconfirmed transaction on the network. Multiple miners will all confirm transactions that are added to the block, achieving a consensus that the coin has only been spent once in one transaction. This verification is the most important job that miners undertake. Even though only one miner will get the 'block reward', the whole network weighs in to verify the transactions en-masse.

ERC20 tokens - Ethereum Request for Comments. The primary protocol on the Ethereum network that allows anyone to create their own crypto token or run a smart contract. The majority of ICO fundraisers were done in this way, and there are now over 200,000 ERC20 tokens. Ethereum has other protocols too, such as ERC165, ERC721, ERC223, ERC621, ERC777 and ERC827.

Ethereum - Also known as the Ethereum virtual machine (EVM) because it can run smart contracts. ETH is its native coin, and smart contract designers pay a small 'gas fee' for using the secure, decentralised, computational power of the network. Ethereum is the first and still favoured protocol for issuing tokens and conducting ICO fundraising. Long-awaited, 2020 sees the release of Ethereum 2.0, with a new programming language and a controversial switch from proof-of-work to proof-of-stake.

Exchange wallet - A cryptocurrency wallet held on a live crypto exchange. The least secure method of storing your coins. Just because the company may be significant and reliable doesn't make it any less of an attack vector for hackers. If your individual account details are compromised, you can quickly lose your coins. If you insist on leaving your coins on an exchange, be sure to activate 2FA at the very least, and be aware of phishing attempts, primarily via email.

FATF (Financial Action Task Force) - Worldwide organisation with a mandate for preventing money laundering. Most western governments fall in with their recommendations.

Fiat - Our Pounds Sterling, Dollars, Yen and Pesos. From the Latin, meaning 'It shall be done'. All Fiat currencies have eventually hyper-inflated and collapsed throughout history due to government spending and devaluing of the coin. The oldest still in use is the British Pound Sterling.

Fintech - A Financial Technology company or application.

FOMO – Fear of Missing Out. A gut reaction that must be resisted at all costs.

Forex - Foreign exchange (of Fiat currencies).

FUD – Fear, Uncertainty and Doubt. News, often fake, designed to create negative feelings about a coin or product. The term has been around since at least 1975.

Fundamental investor - An investor, like the famous Warren Buffet, that only invests in a company based on its viability. He is more concerned with the real facts and long-term success than the hype - usually the opposite of a Technical Investor, who looks primarily at charts and market sentiment.

Gas - Unit of payment in the Ethereum network, in Ether, for payment of a smart contract or money transfer implementation.

Genesis block - The first-ever block of Bitcoin (or any other coin) that was mined by Satoshi and contained the Times headline.

Geo-redundancy - signifies a computer system operating at two or more geographical locations as a redundancy, in case the primary system fails due to any reason.

Gold standard - A system once used by western governments to guarantee that they held an equal amount of gold to the value of Fiat notes in circulation. Abandoned by Richard Nixon in 1974, it understandably caused a lack of trust in the US Dollar. For a while, the Swiss Franc became the world currency. Many people think that the money in their pocket is backed by real assets, especially gold, but it is not.

The Halving (or Halvening) - An event in the Bitcoin blockchain (and others such as Litecoin) that reduces the block mining reward by half.

The theory goes that reducing supply will increase the price per coin and should still allow miners to profit. In the case of Bitcoin, this happens every 210,000 blocks, approximately every four years. The latest, Bitcoin's third, was on May 11th, 2020, and reduced the reward from 12.5 Bitcoins per 10-minute block mined to 6.25 Bitcoins. Similarly, Litecoin halvenings happen every 840,000 blocks, which is also approximately every 4 years, because Litecoin blocks take about 2.5 minutes to mine. There is generally a great deal of retail investor buy-in interest in the weeks running up to the event, with big players selling high just afterwards. Historical data shows the price then dropping slightly before going up to more significant highs...so far.

Hard fork - Changes to a cryptocurrency's code that don't gain 100% consensus. The 'new' coin carries on as usual but via a new blockchain. Users can decide which they prefer, so it's a very democratic method.

Hardware Security Modules (HSM) - The usual banking solution. Not good enough to compete with private crypto keys.

Hash function - Algorithm that generates an un-crackable result from several inputs. Used to lock together each block securely and make the Blockchain secure and irreversible.

Hash rate - A unit measuring the total amount of processing power on a blockchain network. The Bitcoin network was using around 4 exahashes at time of writing. That's 1,000,000,000,000,000,000, or one Quintillion, calculations per second.

HODL – Hold on for Dear Life. A term for HOLD invented by die-hard coin owners that never intend to sell and are in it for the long run.

Hyper-inflation - When a currency decreases in value extremely fast, causing it to be near worthless. This is due to government spending or dilution of the money supply. It's not a thing of the past, either. Many countries, including Zimbabwe, Argentina, Venezuela, Syria and Lebanon have recently suffered this fate, with the country's citizens taking the fall. And now Cuba has been forced to revalue its currency too.

ICO - Initial Coin Offering. Issuing new cryptocurrencies for sale on the open market, usually facilitated by the Ethereum network. Some of these have broken Security issuance laws, and worldwide governments are cracking down.

IEO - Initial Exchange Offering. Issuing new cryptocurrencies for sale on a cryptocurrency exchange. The exchange supposedly takes responsibility for checking the legality and viability of the token...if they're a legal exchange, to begin with. And there is an immediate aftermarket for the coin. Securities laws still apply.

KYC - Know Your Customer. Policies by which companies deal with money laundering and terrorist financing laws and monitor unusual transactions across their customer base.

Litecoin - early clone of Bitcoin designed to be faster to transact with.

Mining - Process by which transactions on a blockchain ledger are processed and verified. There are at least a million miners plugged into the Bitcoin network, either individually or via a mining pool.

Mining difficulty – Bitcoin's code adjusts the difficulty of mining on the network every 2016 blocks (2 weeks), by making the block puzzle-solving harder or easier. This is directly related to the total Hash Power of the network, to achieve a specific mining target (e.g. 10 minutes per block). So whatever the participation by miners, the network will never grind to a halt.

Moon – Or 'when moon'. Speculatory statement asking when a coin price is going to take off and 'go to the moon'. Often accompanied by a rocket symbol, though if I see a rocket symbol, personally I just automatically think 'scam'.

Multi-Party Computation (MPC) - split private keys and multisig.
Multisig - Most wallets are signed by one person or private key. Others require multiple signatures for added security.

Node – Any computer or miner that contains a complete and up to date copy of the Blockchain. This is critical to make a distributed ledger impossible-to-hack. Bitcoin currently has nearly 100,000 nodes, and anyone can operate one.

P2P - Peer to peer. Bitcoin transactions are P2P which means directly from me to you without any third party getting involved or having to be trusted.

Payment token - A cryptocurrency used primarily for making payments rather than providing utility or smart contracting, or as a speculative asset.

PEP - Politically Exposed Person for the purposes of AML checks. This is anyone in public office that could potentially be responsible for wrongly spending their budgets, among other things.

Phone wallet - Cryptocurrency wallet software on a mobile phone. Prone to attack by hackers due to its internet-connected nature, but handy for carrying Crypto to make modest payments. Not to be used to hold your entire stash.

Private seed phrase - A collection of up to 24 English language words to depict a private key and designed to be easier to remember or write down. This can be produced easily from a hexadecimal private key, or vice versa, using software. There is a link in the next section.

Proof of work POW - A blockchain distributed ledger that contains a permanent record of all transactions, called proof-of-work. Currently the most secure type of Blockchain, due to the sheer computational power required to secure it. Generally speaking, the bigger the Blockchain, the more difficult it is to gain control.

Proof of stake and staking POS – Alternative to the energy-hungry (but more secure) proof-of-work mining method used by Bitcoin and others. To participate, miners must lock up coins on the Blockchain, gaining them the right to a percentage of the rewards. A miner with a stake of 1% of all the coins will receive 1% of the mining reward for verifying transactions. There is, however, an inherent risk where simply by owning more coins, the stakeholders could potentially exert undue influence, and this makes it potentially less secure. Plus, its very stakeholders become a target for government or outside control.

However, it's an open debate, and Ethereum 2.0 will switch from POW to POS in 2020.

Public and private keys - Your cryptocurrency wallet is made up of both a public and private key. The latter is required to make transactions and must be kept safe. The public key can be given out for others to pay into, or to buy Crypto on an exchange. Note that once someone has been given your public key, they can look up all your transactions at that address on the Blockchain, if it isn't a privacy coin.

Pump and Dump – Where single or multiple buyers buy a lot of one particular token in an attempt to increase the price, then sell at the top of the market, which in turn will decrease the price.

Rekt – Meaning that you made significant losses on a trade or coin. "I got Rekd on Einsteinium" (yes that was a real coin).

Satoshi Nakamoto - The anonymous man, woman, group, government or mafia organisation that might or might not have invented Bitcoin. While it could be any person or organisation because the identity is anonymous, it's widely thought to be one person due to an analysis of his writings, among other things. Many point to PGP developer Hal Finney, a California computer scientist who sadly passed away from ALS in 2014 and to Nick Szabo, computer scientist and scholar. Other people have claimed to be Satoshi, most famously Australian computer scientist Craig Wright, but have been unable to prove it and have quickly been debunked.

Satoshis SAT – The smallest unit of Bitcoin representing 100,000,000th of a Bitcoin.

SE chip - Secure Element chip. One of the custom chips contained in hardware cold storage wallets.

Security token - A cryptocurrency or blockchain token that is determined as acting like a regular security, and thus has a speculative nature and expectation of price increase, profits or dividends.

Sharding – Breaking data into smaller pieces for computation and storage for speed and security. Will be used in Ethereum 2.

Shill – Promoting a coin to increase the public interest and price. Usually used as an unfavourable comment, not a positive one.

Shitcoin – As the name suggests, one with no value or use. Often pumped and dumped permanently.

Smart contracts - Secure contracts for mostly simple transactions that exist on a blockchain, particularly Ethereum, without the need for any third-party oversight. A simple example would be; person A receives payment, and person B automatically receives product or service. The contract is open on the Blockchain and, while it can be cancelled before execution, once executed, it cannot be reversed. This gives 100% security to the participants. More and more applications are being written, from insurance policies and pay-outs to gambling and real estate ownership.

Smurfing – I know. No, this is nothing to do with 'Papa Smurf'. Smurfing is the term given to repeated multiple payments of the same amount, or repeated payments just under the reporting threshold, which is usually about $10,000 or the equivalent thereof. This activity is deemed suspicious.

Soft fork - Changes, updates or additions to a blockchain code which receive consensus of the community.

Stable coins - A cryptocurrency supposedly linked to other assets such as Fiat currency, stocks or other investments, which give it a stable price. This enables it to be used as an electronic medium of exchange, which is both faster than getting Fiat into the system and not subject to wild swings in price. However, one of the world's most significant, US Dollar Tether (USDT), is subject to a total lack of auditing and the theft by its centralised management (BitFinex) of 850 million dollars. In a world moving towards negative interest rates, it is difficult to see how a purely cash-backed stable coin can remain viable. Some use less liquid assets such as real estate, but they are not really fit for purpose.

Technical investor - A person who watches the charts and market sentiment to make investment decisions. Less concerned with being a 'Fundamental' investor. Hard to get right in the world of Cryptocurrency because there are dominant players that can move the (relatively small) market with a single trade. This is very hard to predict.

Trustless – Somewhat a misnomer as it sounds like 'not to be trusted'. However, it means that there is no need to trust a third party in a P2P or decentralised transaction, giving absolute certainty and security to the individuals involved. Removing the middleman is one of the most spectacular cost and time-saving benefits that this technology brings.

Utility token - A crypto token that has real utility and function, rather than speculation or payment alone (although a token can be two or all three of these things). This might be to pay exchange fees or give exclusive rights of access to a company's products for the holder.

Whale – A substantial investor with significant holdings and the ability to sometimes move the market.

15. SOME USEFUL LINKS, APPS, NEWSLETTERS AND WEBSITES

Coin Cap app – I love this app, designed by Shapeshift, and headed up by one of the big names and positive voices in the space, libertarian Eric Vorhees. Multiple coins in your list light up green or red as the market flips between buying and selling. I stare at it for long periods of time and you actually begin to get a sense of what direction the market is going in. Watch the money flow between alts and Bitcoin. You'll see what I mean. Apart from that, it's the best looking app out there to keep tally of prices and daily volumes.

Bitcoin White Paper - Satoshi Nakamoto, Oct 31st, 2008, releases the original Bitcoin white paper: "I've been working on a new electronic cash system that's fully peer-to-peer, with no trusted third party."

http://www.bitcoin.org/bitcoin.pdf

Blockchain explorer – look up Bitcoin transactions and wallets at www.blockchain.com

Ethereum blockchain explorer – For Ether transactions go to www.eth-erscan.io

Bitcoin alterations (BIP code list) - https://github.com/bitcoin/bips

Bitcoin.org – Website representing the original Bitcoin Core (BTC)

Bitcoin.com – Website representing the Bitcoin Cash (BCH) hard fork. Domain is owned by so-called 'Bitcoin Jesus', Roger Ver. Because the name 'Bitcoin' can't be trademarked, anyone can use it. Therefore, it's worth mentioning that this does not represent the views of the Bitcoin community as a whole, nor is he connected to BTC in any way.

Mnemonic seed phrase convertor – Generate a private key from a phrase of words or vice versa. https://iancoleman.io/bip39/

Nulltx.com – Excellent and credible daily crypto news outlet. One of the best free sources out there. Well worth subscribing. https://nulltx.com

Cambridge University research. Excellent detailed and credible. Search 2nd Global Cryptoasset Benchmarking Study. Or; https://www.jbs.cam.ac.uk/fileadmin/user_upload/research/centres/alternative-finance/downloads/2019-09-ccaf-2nd-global-cryptoasset-benchmarking.pdf

Database of every Bitcoin public key - https://lbc.cryptoguru.org/dio/

Bitcoin Wiki – over 1200 pages of info https://en.bitcoin.it/wiki/Main_Page

Wallets - Blockchain Wallet, Litewallet, CoPay, Jaxx, Mycelium

Cold storage devices – www.trezor.io www.ledger.com

Blockfolio App – Great for tracking your portfolio and curating news relating to your coins.

Coincap App – Shows market price and volumes for all Crypto. Excellent visualisation. Watching the money move around the market as cryptocurrencies flash green or red (up or down) is quite addictive.

Defipulse.com and Defiprime.com – excellent sources of up to date information on the Decentralised Finance world.

BTC News App – Decent, credible, roundup of all the news.

The Pomp Newsletter and podcast – by Anthony Pompliano https://pomp.substack.com

Untold Stories Podcast by legendary Crypto luminary Charlie Shrem. Charlie, with backing from the Winklevoss twins, started Bit Instant in 2011, the first really professional exchange. But he was sentenced to jail for two years because it was found that some of the crypto had gone on to be used on the Silk road marketplace. He is now one of the top five figures in the space, and a hero to many, including myself - https://blockworksgroup.io/untold-stories-podcast

Crypto. IQ. News and investment advice, also by Charlie Shrem. Worth the subscription price, but some elements are free anyway – www.cryptoiq.co

Bankless newsletter by Ryan Sean Adams - https://bankless.substack.com

The Block crypto news - https://www.theblockcrypto.com

Dead coins – www.coinopsy.com

Lastly, I'm on Twitter as Andrew Smales (I think there are only two of us in the world) - @Andrew_Smales

Printed in Great Britain
by Amazon

60928224R10058